Oracle Certification Prep

Study Guide for

1Z0-144: Oracle Database 11g:

Program with PL/SQL

Matthew Morris

Study Guide for Oracle Database 11g: Program with PL/SQL (Exam 1Z0-144) Rev 1.2

ISBN-13: 978-1478217992
ISBN-10: 1478217995

Table of Contents

What to Expect from the Test

The test consists of 80 multiple choice or multiple answer questions. The passing score listed on Oracle Education at this time is 65%, but as with all Oracle certification tests, they note it is subject to change. This test contains a significant number of questions that contain one or more exhibits.

As you would expect, in this exam you're going to be looking at a significant number of PL/SQL constructs. A reasonable percentage will ask you to look at a PL/SQL procedure, function, or package and then pick one answer from a list that is true (or false) about the construct. Other questions might ask what will happen when you invoke a subprogram or what is required in order for the subprogram to work properly.

Other items will involve questions about valid syntax or what can or cannot be performed using a package, procedure or function. You'll also need to recognize what PL/SQL constructs are capable of, understand how variables and parameters work, how to determine when something can be referenced, and be able to differentiate between legal and illegal syntax. You need a firm grounding in PL/SQL in order to do well on the exam. You'll need to be able to parse PL/SQL in your head and work out what it does – often flipping back and forth between an exhibit and a question while doing so.

Read the questions completely, examine the code carefully and look at all of the answer before making your choice. That said, pay close attention to the time. With ninety minutes to answer eighty questions, you have less than sixty-eight seconds per question. A number of the exhibits were not really required to answer the question – they showed the table structure that was referenced by a PL/SQL subprogram rather than the code itself. The text on the exam says to look at the exhibit and then read the question, but I highly recommend doing the opposite. If you can answer a question without looking at a given exhibit, then you will have saved yourself some time. You'll need it. I doubt that many people taking the test will find themselves with lots of spare time at the end and I guarantee that a number will run out of time before they run out of questions. Any questions left unanswered are automatically wrong.

What to Expect from this Study Guide

This document is built around the subject matter topics that Oracle Education has indicated will appear on the 1Z0-144 exam. I've gathered together material from several Oracle documentation sources and created numerous code examples. Together they should help to familiarize you with the PL/SQL concepts, logic, and syntax that you will need to answer the questions you're likely to see on the test. Be aware that reading this guide is not going to make you into a PL/SQL programmer, nor is it supposed to. There are books available that are designed to improve your skills and knowledge as a PL/SQL developer. This guide is designed to help you to pass the 1Z0-144 certification exam.

In this book, I am assuming that you already have some experience coding in PL/SQL. If you do not, you should have at least one other source of information and more to the point, you should practice writing PL/SQL code before seeking this certification. No book, in and of itself, is a substitute for hands-on development experience. Since Oracle has made the Oracle XE version of its database free to download and use, there is no reason why anyone who wants to learn to code in PL/SQL cannot get that hands-on experience. Also, when using this guide, do not simply read the text, glance at the code long enough to say to yourself 'Yep, that looks like code' and then move on to the next paragraph. The code is the meat of this exam. You must understand both the syntax and the logic of the PL/SQL functionality that will be on the exam.

The goal of this guide is to present to you the concepts and information most likely to be the subject of test questions, and to do so in a very compact format that will allow you to read through it more than once to reinforce the information. If much of the information presented in this guide is completely new to you then you need to supplement this guide with other source of study materials to gain a firm understanding of PL/SQL fundamentals. If you have a reasonable grounding in the basic concepts and are comfortable with writing PL/SQL code, then this book will help to reinforce your knowledge in the areas you will need the most. If you don't have **any** experience with PL/SQL at all, the compressed format of this guide is not likely to be the best method for learning. It is possible (barely) that it will provide you with sufficient information to pass the test, but you will have major deficiencies as a PL/SQL developer.

Additional Study Resources

The companion website to this series is www.oraclecertificationprep.com. The site contains many additional resources that can be used to study for this exam (and others). From the entry page of the website, click on the 'Exams' button, and then select the link for this test. The Exam Details page contains links to the following information sources:

- Applicable Oracle documentation.
- Third-party books relevant to the exam.
- White papers and articles on Oracle Learning Library on topics covered in the exam.
- Articles on the Web that may be useful for the exam.

The website will <u>never</u> link to unauthorized content such as brain dumps or illegal content such as copyrighted material made available without the consent of the author. I cannot guarantee the accuracy of the content links. While I have located the data and scanned it to ensure that it is relevant to the given exam, I did not write it and have not proofread it from a technical standpoint. The material on the Oracle Learning Library is almost certain to be completely accurate and most of the other links come from highly popular Oracle support websites and are created by experienced Oracle professionals.

I recommend that you use more than one source of study materials whenever you are preparing for a certification. Reading information presented from multiple different viewpoints can help to give you a more complete picture of any given topic. The links on the website can help you to do this. Fully understanding the information covered in this certification is not just valuable so that getting a passing score is more likely – it will also help you in your career. I guarantee that in the long run, any knowledge you gain while studying for this certification will provide more benefit to you than any piece of paper or line on your resume.

Practice Questions

The guides in the Oracle Certification Prep series do not contain example questions. The format that they are designed around is not really compatible. The concise format used for the study guides means that adding a reasonable number of questions would nearly double the size of the guides themselves. However, because practice questions have been a common request from readers of my books, I have created a series of practice tests for the exams. The practice tests are available from the companion website listed in the previous section of this guide. They are not free, but the price is a fraction of that charged by other vendors for Oracle certification practice tests.

Unlike much of the material advertised online, these tests are not brain dumps. All of the tests are original content that I developed. Using these exams will not endanger your certification status with the Oracle certification program. I submit each test to the certification team after I finish developing it so that they can verify that they do not contain illicit material. These tests serve as an inexpensive means for any certification candidate that wants to determine how successful their preparation has been before scheduling the real exam.

As a purchaser of this study guide, you can use the following promotional code to get $2.00 off the purchase price of the practice exam for 1Z0-144: **144_CDIWTF.**

The tests are available at the following URL:

http://oraclecertificationprep.com/apex/f?p=OCPSG:Practice_Tests

Introduction to PL/SQL

Explain the need for PL/SQL

Structured Query Language (SQL) is a very powerful language with a great deal of flexibility in retrieving data from the database or inserting & manipulating data. However, SQL has no robust procedural element to allow it to apply logical processing to data retrieval or manipulation. The DECODE and CASE statements in the SQL language provide for a very basic level of conditional processing, but fall short of even moderately complex requirements.

PL/SQL adds the processing power of a procedural language to the data-manipulating capability of SQL. PL/SQL provides procedural constructs, such as conditional statements and loops that cannot be performed using standard SQL. It provides the ability to declare variables and constants, control program flow, define subprograms, and handle runtime errors. Complex problems can be broken down into discrete subprograms, which can be reused in multiple applications. SQL data manipulation language (DML) statements can be directly entered inside PL/SQL blocks, and it is possible to use subprograms to execute data definition language (DDL) and Data Control Language (DCL) statements.

Explain the benefits of PL/SQL

- **Tight Integration with SQL** -- PL/SQL is highly integrated with SQL and allows you to make use of all of the SQL capabilities. You can execute SQL data manipulation, cursor control, and transaction control statements. PL/SQL can use existing SQL functions, operators, and pseudocolumns. PL/SQL fully supports SQL data types without any need for conversion. It's possible to run a SQL query and process the rows of the result set one at a time.
- **High Performance** -- Through the use of collections, bind variables, and cached programs, PL/SQL can reduce network traffic, SQL parse operations and other overhead, improving performance on the database.

- **High Productivity** -- PL/SQL has many features that save designing and debugging time, and it is the same in all environments.
- **Portability** -- You can run PL/SQL applications on any operating system and platform where Oracle Database runs.
- **Scalability** -- PL/SQL stored subprograms increase scalability by centralizing application processing on the database server.
- **Manageability** -- You need to maintain only a single copy of a subprogram on the database server, rather than one copy on each client system.
- **Support for Object-Oriented Programming** -- PL/SQL supports object-oriented programming with Abstract Data Types.
- **Support for Developing Web Applications** -- It is possible to create applications that generate web pages directly from the database.
- **Support for Developing Server Pages** -- PL/SQL Server Pages (PSPs) allow web pages with dynamic content and are an alternative to PL/SQL HTML coding that creates a web page one line at a time.

Identify the different types of PL/SQL blocks

A block is the basic unit of a PL/SQL program. PL/SQL blocks group related declarations and statements. The four keywords that define a PL/SQL block are: DECLARE, BEGIN, EXCEPTION, and END. They are used to make up the three sections of a block:

- **DECLARE** -- The declarative section begins with the keyword DECLARE and ends when the executable section starts. This section is optional and is used to declare variables, constants, cursors, and user-defined data types.
- **BEGIN** -- The executable section of the block starts with the BEGIN keyword and ends with the END keyword. This is the only mandatory section of a PL/SQL block and must contain at least one statement. The executable section can contain an effectively

unlimited number of PL/SQL blocks. This section contains the meat of the PL/SQL program.

- **EXCEPTION** -- The exception-handling section is used to trap and handle run-time errors. It begins with the EXCEPTION keyword and ends with the END keyword. This section is optional.

The three section keywords are not followed by a semicolon. However, the END keyword is. Also, all SQL and PL/SQL statements in the block must terminate with a semicolon.

An example of a basic PL/SQL block would be:

```
DECLARE
  v_temp    NUMBER;
BEGIN
  v_temp := 1;

EXCEPTION
  WHEN OTHERS THEN
    DBMS_OUTPUT.PUT_LINE('This block will never create an
exception');
    DBMS_OUTPUT.PUT_LINE('But if one occurred, this would
trap it.');
END;
```

There are two broad types of PL/SQL blocks:

Anonymous Blocks -- These are unnamed PL/SQL blocks. They may be executed immediately from within SQL*Plus, SQL*Developer or a similar tool. Anonymous blocks might also be declared in-line in an application where they should be executed. They are not stored in the database and are passed to the PL/SQL engine to be compiled and executed each time the block is run. Anonymous blocks cannot be called from other PL/SQL blocks. Anonymous blocks can be submitted to an interactive tool like SQL*Plus or embedded in an Oracle Precompiler or OCI program. An anonymous block is compiled each time it is loaded into memory in three stages:

1. **Syntax checking** -- PL/SQL syntax is checked, and a parse tree is generated.
2. **Semantic checking** -- Type checking and further processing on the parse tree.
3. **Code generation** – The compiled code is created.

Subprograms -- A subprogram is a named PL/SQL block that is stored in the data dictionary. Because they are named and available in the dictionary tables, named blocks can be invoked repeatedly. Subprograms can contain parameters, and the values of these can be different for each invocation. There are two types of subprograms: Procedures and Functions. The primary difference between the two is that a function always returns a value when called. The other differences will be discussed in further detail later.

Triggers -- A trigger is a special kind of PL/SQL anonymous block that can be defined to fire before or after SQL statements. They can fire either on a statement level or for each row that is affected. It is also possible to define INSTEAD OF triggers or system triggers.

Output messages in PL/SQL

The actions performed inside of a PL/SQL block are not displayed to the console. Unless specifically coded to generate output, the most complex procedure will generate nothing except a message indicating the block completed (or an error message if something goes wrong). To generate output for debugging or status messages, the most commonly used method is the PUT_LINE procedure of the DBMS_OUTPUT package. The DBMS_OUTPUT package is typically used for debugging, or for displaying messages and reports to the console. Alternately, the PUT_LINE Procedure enables you to place information in a buffer that can be read by another PL/SQL block. In a separate block, you can display the buffered information by calling the GET_LINE or GET_LINES Procedure.

Before output will be displayed to the console, the buffer that accepts these messages must be enabled. The buffer status determines whether or not to display the output of PUT_LINE commands in SQL*Plus. The DBMS_OUTPUT line length limit is 32767 bytes. The buffer is most commonly enabled by issuing the following command (the SIZE parameter is optional):

```
SET SERVEROUTPUT ON
```

or

```
SET SERVEROUTPUT ON SIZE 1000000
```

You can turn the buffer off with the command:

```
SET SERVEROUTPUT OFF
```

It should be noted that messages buffered using DBMS_OUTPUT are not actually sent until the sending subprogram or trigger completes. It is not possible to flush the output during the execution of a procedure. If you have a procedure that contains debugging messages, but is in an endless loop -- you will never see the debugging information. The following example shows the DBMS_OUTPUT.PUT_LINE procedure used to display debugging information for a procedure:

```
DECLARE
  v_index    NUMBER;
BEGIN
  v_index := 1;
  DBMS_OUTPUT.PUT_LINE('Starting the loop');
  DBMS_OUTPUT.NEW_LINE;

  WHILE v_index < 6 LOOP
    DBMS_OUTPUT.PUT_LINE('v_index: ' || v_index);
    v_index := v_index + 1;
  END LOOP;

  DBMS_OUTPUT.NEW_LINE;
  DBMS_OUTPUT.PUT_LINE('Loop ended');
END;
```

```
Starting the loop

v_index: 1
v_index: 2
v_index: 3
v_index: 4
v_index: 5

Loop ended
```

Declaring PL/SQL Variables

Recognize valid and invalid identifiers

PL/SQL lets you declare variables and constants for use within a block. Once declared, it is possible to use them wherever an expression could be used. During the execution of a PL/SQL block, the values of variables can change, but the values of constants cannot. Variables and constants must adhere to the following rules for user-defined identifiers:

- It must be composed of characters from the database character set
- Can be either ordinary (non-quoted) or quoted

Ordinary User-Defined identifiers

Non-quoted identifiers must meet the following restrictions:

- Must begin with a letter
- Can include letters, digits, a dollar sign ($), a number sign (#), or an underscore (_).
- Is not a reserved word.
- Cannot exceed 30 bytes.

Examples of acceptable non-quoted identifiers:

- n
- x2
- SSN#
- v_count
- FirstName
- Big$$

Examples of unacceptable ordinary non-quoted identifiers:

- M&M
- v-amount
- teeter/totter
- user id

Quoted User-Defined Identifiers

Quoted user-defined identifiers are enclosed by double quotation marks. Between the double quotation marks, any characters from the database character set are allowed except double quotation marks, new line characters, and null characters.

Examples of acceptable quoted identifiers:

- "A+B"
- "first name"
- "on/off"
- "manager(s)"
- "*** comment ***"

A quoted user-defined identifier is case-sensitive, with one exception. If a quoted user-defined identifier is a valid ordinary user-defined identifier, then the double quotation marks are optional. If the quotes are left off, then the identifier is case-insensitive.

Naming Conventions

While it is possible to call variables anything at all (so long as you follow the rules above), in practice it is much better to use a logical naming convention. A common naming convention is to prefix variables with 'v_', constants with 'c_' and parameter names with 'p_'. I've worked for shops that went further, prefixing number variables with 'n_', varchar2 variables with 'v_', boolean variables with 'b_' and so forth. The specific naming convention is less important than picking one convention and following it. Maintaining PL/SQL code that has been written using a standard naming convention is much easier than one that has been written haphazardly.

List the uses of variables

Variables act as buckets to store values that are either unknown at the start of the PL/SQL block or might change during execution of the block. Values that are known at the time of the declaration section and will not change should be created as constants rather than variables. They can be used to store values originating from several different sources:

- **Declaration Section** -- Variables can be created in the declaration section and simultaneously assigned an initial value. In the declaration section, the variable will be given a name, a type, and depending on the data type possibly given a set storage space.
- **Executable Section** -- Variable that have been defined in the declaration section (or global variables defined in a package body) may be explicitly assigned a value in the executable section of the block. Variables created in the declaration section and not given an initial value will be NULL until assigned a value.

- **SQL INTO targets** -- Variables can be used as the target of s SELECT INTO statement. The output of the SQL statement will become the value of the variable(s).
- **PL/SQL RETURN target** -- Variables can be used to hold the return value of a function or procedure.
- **PL/SQL Parameters** -- Variables can be used as the source for IN parameters in PL/SQL subprograms, or hold the output of an OUT parameter in subprograms, or both for IN/OUT parameters.

Declare and initialize variables

Declaring a variable allocates storage space to hold a value, specifies the data type, and provides a name so that it can be referenced. Variables must be declared before they can be referenced. Declarations can appear in the declarative part of any block, subprogram, or package. The name and data type of the variable is always specified during the declaration. Some data types also require a storage size, and for most data types, the declaration can also specify an initial value. The name of the variable must be a valid identifier. A variable can be declared as any PL/SQL data type. The PL/SQL data types include the SQL data types plus several more that are specific to PL/SQL. It is also possible to create user-defined data types. There are four broad classes of data types:

- **Scalar** -- Scalar types contain no internal components. Examples are the SQL data types, and the PL/SQL data types: BOOLEAN, PLS_INTEGER, BINARY_INTEGER, and REF CURSOR.
- **Composite** -- Composite data types contain internal components. Examples include collections and records.
- **Reference** – Reference data types contain pointers to a storage location.
- **LOB** – LOB data types contain values called locators that specify the location of large objects.

The base syntax for declaring a variable is:

```
identifier [CONSTANT] datatype [NOT NULL] [:= | DEFAULT
expr];
```

An example of a PL/SQL block declaring several variables is:

```
DECLARE
  v_serial      NUMBER;          -- SQL data type
  v_part_name   VARCHAR2(20);    -- SQL data type
  v_in_stock    BOOLEAN;         -- PL/SQL-only data type
  v_price       NUMBER(6,2);     -- SQL data type
  v_part_desc   VARCHAR2(50);    -- SQL data type
  v_count       PLS_INTEGER  NOT NULL  := 0;    -- PL/SQL-only
data type
BEGIN
  NULL;
END;
/
```

Constants have the same naming restrictions as variables. In addition, a constant declaration has two additional requirements. The declaration must include the keyword CONSTANT and supply an initial value of the constant (which is effectively its permanent value.) The following example declares three constants:

```
DECLARE
  v_limit     CONSTANT NUMBER  := 1000; -- SQL data type
  v_port      CONSTANT INTEGER := 1541; -- SQL data type
  v_open      CONSTANT BOOLEAN := TRUE; -- PL/SQL-only data
type
BEGIN
  NULL;
END;
/
```

Constants are always assigned a value when declared. When declaring a variable, the initial value is optional unless specified as NOT NULL. For variable assignments made in the declaration section of a block or subprogram, the initial value is assigned to the variable or constant every time the block executes. For declarations made in a package specification, the initial value is assigned to the variable or constant once per session. You can use either the assignment operator (:=) or the keyword DEFAULT, followed by an expression to assign a value at declaration. The expression can include constants and/or variables if they have been previously declared. The following example assigns initial values to the constants and variables that it declares.

```
DECLARE
  v_reg_pay   NUMBER            := 37.50;
  v_ot_mod    CONSTANT NUMBER := 1.5;
  v_ot_pay    NUMBER            := v_reg_pay * v_ot_mod;
BEGIN
  NULL;
END;
/
```

Use bind variables

Bind variables are not created in the declarative section of a PL/SQL block but rather in the host environment where the block is running. For that reason, they are sometimes referred to as host variables. Variables declared within a PL/SQL block have scope only within that block. Once the block has completed running, the memory associated with the variables is released and the variables are no longer accessible. Bind variables, however, continue to be accessible even after the block has completed. Bind variables therefore can be accessed and used by multiple PL/SQL blocks. The variables can be passed in and out of PL/SQL blocks as run-time variables. The VARIABLE command is used to create a variable in SQL*Plus or SQL*Developer. The following example creates a bind variable:

```
VARIABLE bv_return_val  VARCHAR2(20)
VARIABLE bv_return_code NUMBER
```

The above bind variables can then be referenced from within a PL/SQL block by preceding the variable name with a colon:

```
BEGIN
  SELECT emp_job
  INTO   :bv_return_val
  FROM   employees
  WHERE  emp_id=18;

  :bv_return_code := 0;
EXCEPTION
  WHEN OTHERS THEN
    :bv_return_code := 1;
END;
```

It's now possible to use the PRINT command from SQL*Plus or SQL*Developer to view the values in the variables. Had they been PL/SQL variables rather than bind variables, they would have been undefined once the block had completed.

```
PRINT bv_return_val
BV_RETURN_VAL
---
Mgr

PRINT bv_return_code

BV_RETURN_CODE
-
0
```

List and describe various data types using the %TYPE attribute

PL/SQL variables are often used to store data pulled from tables in the database. When this is the case, the PL/SQL variable must be of the correct data type and size to hold the value being assigned to it. When this is not the case, or if the column changes type or increases in size, it will likely generate a PL/SQL error when the code is executed.

The %TYPE attribute lets you declare a variable to be of the same data type as a previously declared variable or column. It is not required that you know what that type is when making the assignment (or ever for that matter). If the declaration of the referenced item changes in the future, then the declaration of the referencing item changes to match. The syntax for using the %TYPE declaration is:

```
referencing_item referenced_item%TYPE;
```

The referencing item inherits the following from the referenced item:

- Data type and size
- Constraints (unless the referenced item is a column)

A variable using %TYPE does not inherit the initial value of the referenced item. If the referencing item specifies NOT NULL or inherits NOT NULL from the referenced item, an initial value must be specified. However, note that PL/SQL variables declared using %TYPE <u>do not</u> inherit the NOT NULL constraint from database columns. %TYPE is ideally suited for declaring variables to hold database column values. The syntax for declaring a variable of the same type as a column is:

```
variable_name table_name.column_name%TYPE;
```

The following example shows using the %TYPE attribute to declare a variable using an existing column.

```
DECLARE
  v_last_name   employees.emp_last%TYPE;
BEGIN
  SELECT emp_last
  INTO   v_last_name
  FROM   employees
  WHERE  emp_id = 9;

  DBMS_OUTPUT.PUT_LINE('v_last_name = ' || v_last_name);
END;

anonymous block completed
v_last_name = Storm
```

The following example uses the %TYPE attribute to set the commission and bonus variables to the same data type as the salary variable:

```
DECLARE
  v_salary       NUMBER(6,2);
  v_commission   v_salary%TYPE;
  v_bonus        v_salary%TYPE;
BEGIN
  NULL;
END;
```

Writing Executable Statements

Identify lexical units in a PL/SQL block

The lexical units of PL/SQL are its smallest individual components. These include delimiters, identifiers, literals, and comments.

Delimiters

A delimiter is a character, or character combination, that has a special meaning in PL/SQL. It is not legal to embed any other characters (including whitespace characters) inside a delimiter. Some of the more common delimiters follow. For a complete listing, access the Oracle Database PL/SQL Language Reference.

_ -- Underscore
| -- Vertical bar
:= -- Assignment operator
=> -- Association operator
% -- Attribute indicator
' -- Character string delimiter
. -- Component indicator
|| -- Concatenation operator
( ) -- Expression or list delimiter (begin and end)
: -- Host variable indicator
, -- Item separator
<< >>-- Label delimiter (begin and end)
" -- Quoted identifier delimiter
.. -- Range operator
+ -- Addition operator
- -- Subtraction or negation operator
/ -- Division operator
* -- Multiplication operator
** -- Exponentiation operator
= -- Relational operator (equal)
<> -- Relational operator (not equal)

!= -- Relational operator (not equal)
~= -- Relational operator (not equal)
^= -- Relational operator (not equal)
< -- Relational operator (less than)
> -- Relational operator (greater than)
<= -- Relational operator (less than or equal)
>= -- Relational operator (greater than or equal)
@ -- Remote access indicator
/* */ -- Multiline comment delimiter (begin and end)
-- -- Single-line comment indicator
; -- Statement terminator

Identifiers

Identifiers name individual PL/SQL elements. These elements include the following:

- **Constants** -- A named storage space for a value of a specified data type that does not change.
- **Cursors** -- A pointer to a private SQL area that stores information about processing a specific SQL statement or PL/SQL SELECT INTO statement.
- **Exceptions** -- A named error condition that requires handling.
- **Keywords** -- Words that have special meaning in PL/SQL and which should not be used as non-quoted user identifiers.
- **Labels** -- Identify blocks or statements that can be referenced by other statements in the same scope.
- **Packages** -- A schema object that groups logically related PL/SQL types, variables, constants, subprograms, cursors, and exceptions.
- **Reserved words** -- Words that have special meaning in PL/SQL and which cannot be used as non-quoted user identifiers.
- **Subprograms** -- A named PL/SQL block that can be invoked repeatedly

- **Types** -- A named specification for data that determines its storage format and its valid values and operations.
- **Variables** -- A named storage space for a value of a specified data type that can change.

Every character in an identifier is significant: v_firstname and v_first_name are different identifiers. You must separate adjacent identifiers by one or more whitespace characters or a punctuation character. PL/SQL is case-insensitive for non-quoted identifiers: v_amount is the same identifier as V_AMOUNT.

Reserved words and keywords are identifiers that have special meaning in PL/SQL. Keywords can be used as ordinary user-defined identifiers, but this is not recommended. Reserved words cannot be used as ordinary identifiers. They can be used as quoted identifiers, but this is not recommended. Predefined identifiers are declared in the package STANDARD. An example of a predefined identifier is the exception INVALID_NUMBER. Predefined identifiers can be used as user-defined identifiers, but this is not recommended. A local declaration will override the global declaration

Literals

A literal is a value that is neither represented by an identifier nor calculated from other values. What you see is what you get. For example, 'John' is a character literal and 14.95 is a number literal. However, 2+2 is not a literal, but rather an expression. PL/SQL literals include all SQL literals plus BOOLEAN literals. A BOOLEAN literal is the logical value TRUE, FALSE, or NULL. There are several considerations for character literals:

- Character literals are case-sensitive.
- Whitespace characters are significant.

- If a string literal in a block is broken on more than one line, then the string includes a line-break character. String literals which should not be broken should be concatenated in the PL/SQL block.
- '0' through '9' are not equivalent to the integer literals 0 through 9.
- A character literal with zero characters has the value NULL (which is not the same as a BOOLEAN NULL).
- An ordinary character literal is composed of characters in the database character set.

Comments

Comments in PL/SQL blocks are ignored by the compiler. They are intended to help other application developers understand your source text. Comments are typically used to describe the purpose and use of each code segment. It is also possible to use comments to disable obsolete or unfinished pieces of code or to assist in diagnosis by temporarily disabling certain functions to track down problems.

A single-line comment begins with -- and extends to the end of the line. A multiline comment begins with /*, ends with */, and can span multiple lines. For multiline comments, care must be taken to avoid nested multiline comments. One multiline comment cannot contain another multiline comment. The 'end' delimiter of the nested comment will 'turn off' the comment before the end of the enclosing comment. This will result in an error. The following example shows both types:

```
/* ********************************
   ****   Sample PL/SQL block   ****
   ****   showing comment use   ****
   ******************************** */
DECLARE
  v_count       NUMBER;
  v_total       NUMBER;
BEGIN
  -- Begin processing
  SELECT COUNT(*)
  INTO   v_count
  FROM   employees
  WHERE  job_id = 'IT_PROG';    -- Find # of programmers

  v_total := v_count;
END;
/
```

Whitespace Characters between Lexical Units

Whitespace is ignored by the PL/SQL parser. Adding whitespace characters between lexical units generally makes PL/SQL source text easier to read.

```
DECLARE
  x NUMBER := 10;
  y NUMBER := 5;
  z NUMBER;
BEGIN
  -- valid code but hard to read
  IF x>y THEN z:=x;ELSE z:=y;END IF;

  -- Equivalent and easier to read:
  IF x > y THEN
    z := x;
  ELSE
    z := y;
  END IF;
END;
/
```

Use built-in SQL functions in PL/SQL and sequences in PL/SQL expressions

SQL Functions in PL/SQL Expressions

There are a number of predefined functions available in the Oracle SQL language. Most of these functions can also be used directly in PL/SQL expressions. All of the SQL language functions are available in PL/SQL expressions with the exception of the following function types:

- Aggregate functions (such as MAX and AVG)
- Model functions (such as ITERATION_NUMBER and PREVIOUS)
- Data mining functions (such as CLUSTER_ID and FEATURE_VALUE)
- Analytic functions (such as LAG and RATIO_TO_REPORT)
- Encoding and decoding functions (such as DECODE and DUMP)
- Object reference functions (such as REF and VALUE)
- XML functions (such as APPENDCHILDXML and EXISTSNODE)

Most of the functions above involve multiple rows, which is a key indicator that it's not going to work in a PL/SQL expression. In addition to the above list, there are a few miscellaneous functions that cannot be used, including: CUBE_TABLE, DATAOBJ_TO_PARTITION, LNNVL, NVL2, SYS_CONNECT_BY_PATH, SYS_TYPEID, and WIDTH_BUCKET.

Below is an example of using the SQL functions TO_CHAR, LENGTH, AND SUBSTR in PL/SQL:

```
DECLARE
  v_chardate     VARCHAR2(20);
  v_datelength   NUMBER;
  v_mon          VARCHAR2(5);
BEGIN
  v_chardate    := TO_CHAR(SYSDATE, 'DD-MON-YYYY HH24:MI:SS');
  v_datelength  := LENGTH(v_chardate);
  v_mon         := SUBSTR(v_chardate, 4, 3);

  DBMS_OUTPUT.PUT_LINE('v_chardate:   ' || v_chardate);
  DBMS_OUTPUT.PUT_LINE('v_datelength: ' || v_datelength);
  DBMS_OUTPUT.PUT_LINE('v_mon:        ' || v_mon);

END;
/

v_chardate:   05-JUN-2012 23:15:24
v_datelength: 20
v_mon:        JUN
```

Sequences in PL/SQL Expressions

Prior to Oracle 11g Release 1, in order to access sequence values from within PL/SQL, it was necessary to execute a SQL statement (i.e. SELECT sequence.NEXTVAL FROM dual;). With 11G, you can assign the CURRVAL and NEXTVAL values directly from a PL/SQL expression. The new functionality is available wherever you can use a NUMBER expression. The CURRVAL and NEXTVAL pseudocolumns make the PL/SQL source text easier and clearer. They also improve runtime performance and scalability. Any existing sequence can be accessed using the following notation:

- **sequence_name.CURRVAL** -- Returns the current value of the sequence.
- **sequence_name.NEXTVAL** -- Increments the sequence and returns the new value.

An example of using the new notation follows:

```
CREATE SEQUENCE seq_ocp_temp;

DECLARE
  v_seqval    NUMBER;
BEGIN
  v_seqval := seq_ocp_temp.NEXTVAL;
  DBMS_OUTPUT.PUT_LINE('v_seqval: ' || v_seqval);

  v_seqval := seq_ocp_temp.NEXTVAL;
  DBMS_OUTPUT.PUT_LINE('v_seqval: ' || v_seqval);

  v_seqval := seq_ocp_temp.CURRVAL;
  DBMS_OUTPUT.PUT_LINE('v_seqval: ' || v_seqval);
END;
/

v_seqval: 1
v_seqval: 2
v_seqval: 2
```

Describe when implicit conversions take place and when explicit conversions have to be dealt with

When developing in PL/SQL, it is extremely common to require a conversion from one data type to another. Many if not most of the conversions happen automatically when Oracle detects a need to do so. These operations are called implicit conversions. At other times the PL/SQL block will make use of a conversion function to perform the operation. This is explicit conversion. Oracle is extremely good at detecting the need for conversions and performing them implicitly. However, good programming practice is to minimize the need for implicit conversion and to explicitly convert data type where feasible to provide both maximum control over the operation and better visibility.

Implicit Data Conversion

The database will automatically perform a data type conversion when it makes sense (and is possible... which is part of making sense). There are several rules that apply to implicit data type conversions. Some of the more common are listed below. For a full list, refer to the PL/SQL Language Reference manual.

- On INSERT and UPDATE operations, values are converted to the data type of the affected column.
- On SELECT operations, values are converted from the column data type to the type of the target variable.
- Oracle usually adjusts precision and scale of numeric data to allow for maximum capacity. The numeric data type of PL/SQL operations may differ from the numeric data type of the source columns.
- When a timestamp is converted to a DATE value, the fractional seconds portion of the timestamp value is truncated.
- When comparing a character value with a DATE value, Oracle converts the character data to DATE.
- When a SQL function or operator is called with an argument of the wrong data type, Oracle implicitly converts the argument if possible.
- When making assignments, Oracle converts the value on the right side of the equal sign (=) to the data type of the assignment target on the left.
- During concatenation operations, noncharacter data is converted to CHAR or NCHAR.
- For arithmetic operations or comparisons between character and noncharacter data types, Oracle converts the types to a numeric, date, or rowid, as appropriate.
- In arithmetic operations involving only character data, Oracle converts to a NUMBER.
- User-defined types such as collections cannot be implicitly converted.

Some examples of implicit data conversion are below:

```
DECLARE
  v_pls_integer      PLS_INTEGER  := 15;
  v_number           NUMBER       := 10;
  v_char_num         VARCHAR2(10) := '20';
  v_char_date        VARCHAR2(10) := '03-JAN-06';
  v_num_result       NUMBER;
  v_char_result      VARCHAR2(20);
BEGIN
  -- ** A PLS_INTEGER and a NUMBER have different internal
representations,
  -- ** an implicit conversion is required for the following
arithmetic:
  v_num_result := v_pls_integer + v_number;

  -- ** The result then gets converted into character data
for the below:
  DBMS_OUTPUT.PUT_LINE('v_pls_integer + v_number is: ' ||
v_num_result);


  -- ** The VARCHAR2 value must be converted to NUMBER for
this calculation:
  v_num_result := v_char_num + v_number;

  -- ** The result then gets converted into character data
for the below:
  DBMS_OUTPUT.PUT_LINE('v_char_num + v_number is: ' ||
v_num_result);

  -- ** The VARCHAR2 value must be converted to a DATE to
perform this query:
  SELECT last_name
  INTO   v_char_result
  FROM   hr.employees
  WHERE  hire_date = v_char_date;

  DBMS_OUTPUT.PUT_LINE('v_char_result is: ' ||
v_char_result);
END;

v_pls_integer + v_number is: 25
v_char_num + v_number is: 30
v_char_result is: Hunold
```

Explicit Data Conversion

You can explicitly specify data type conversions using SQL conversion functions. It is Oracle's recommendation that you do so rather than relying on implicit data conversion for the following reasons:

- Code is easier to read when explicit data type conversion functions are used.
- Implicit data type conversion can have a negative impact on performance.
- Implicit conversion depends on the context in which it occurs and may not work the same way in every case.
- Algorithms for implicit conversion are subject to change across software releases and among Oracle products.

Implicit data conversion can only take place when the database recognizes the data being converted as being a valid example of the data it needs to be converted to. For example character data cannot be implicitly converted to a date unless it is in the default date format specified for the database. Likewise character data cannot be implicitly converted to a number if it contains dollar signs or commas. An example of this is shown in the following block:

```
DECLARE
  v_char_num          VARCHAR2(10)  := '$2,436.34';
  v_char_date         VARCHAR2(20)  := 'June 06, 2012';
  v_num_result        NUMBER;
  v_date_result       DATE;
BEGIN
  -- ** This implicit conversion will fail
  BEGIN
    v_num_result := v_char_num;
  EXCEPTION
    WHEN OTHERS THEN
      DBMS_OUTPUT.PUT_LINE('Implicit:   ' || SQLERRM);
  END;

  -- This explicit conversion will succeed
```

```
  v_num_result := TO_NUMBER(v_char_num,
'FML999G999G999G999G990D00');
  DBMS_OUTPUT.PUT_LINE('Explicit:  v_num_result is: ' ||
v_num_result);


DBMS_OUTPUT.PUT_LINE('=========================================
=====');

  -- ** This implicit conversion will fail
  BEGIN
    v_date_result := v_char_date;
  EXCEPTION
    WHEN OTHERS THEN
      DBMS_OUTPUT.PUT_LINE('Implicit:  ' || SQLERRM);
  END;

  -- This explicit conversion will succeed
  v_date_result := TO_DATE(v_char_date, 'Month, DD, YYYY');
  DBMS_OUTPUT.PUT_LINE('Explicit:  v_date_result is: ' ||
v_date_result);
END;

Implicit:  ORA-06502: PL/SQL: numeric or value error:
character to number conversion error
Explicit:  v_num_result is: 2436.34
=============================================
Implicit:  ORA-01858: a non-numeric character was found where
a numeric was expected
Explicit:  v_date_result is: 06-JUN-12
```

Write nested blocks and qualify variables with labels

Nested blocks

When a subprogram is created inside a PL/SQL block, it is called a nested subprogram. Nested subprograms are defined in the declaration section of a PL/SQL block, after all local variables are defined. A nested subprogram can be declared and defined at the same time, or declared initially and defined later in the same block. Declaring the block before defining it is called forward declaration. If nested subprograms in the same PL/SQL block invoke each other, then one requires a forward declaration. Subprograms must be declared before they can be invoked. The forward declaration and the definition must have the same subprogram heading. The example below creates two named subprograms with one being forward declared and invoked by the second, and the second is invoked by the enclosing block:

```
DECLARE
  -- Declare nsp1 (forward declaration):
  PROCEDURE nsp1(p_input  VARCHAR2);

  -- Declare and define nsp2:
  PROCEDURE nsp2(p_input  VARCHAR2) IS
  BEGIN
    DBMS_OUTPUT.PUT_LINE('Printing from nsp2:');
    DBMS_OUTPUT.PUT_LINE('----- ' || p_input);
    nsp1('Calling nsp1 from nsp2');
  END;

  -- Define nsp 1:
  PROCEDURE nsp1(p_input VARCHAR2) IS
  BEGIN
    DBMS_OUTPUT.PUT_LINE('Printing from nsp1:');
    DBMS_OUTPUT.PUT_LINE('----- ' || p_input);
  END;

BEGIN
  nsp2('Calling nsp2 from main block');
END;

Printing from nsp2:
----- Calling nsp2 from main block
Printing from nsp1:
----- Calling nsp1 from nsp2
```

Qualifying variables with labels

Before getting into using labels to qualify variables, it is necessary to understand why there is a need to do so. Variables have both scope and a visibility. The two concepts are similar and related, but not identical:

- **Scope** -- The region of a PL/SQL unit from which a variable can be referenced.
- **Visibility** -- The region of a PL/SQL unit from which a variable can be referenced without a qualifier.

A variable is local to the PL/SQL unit that declares it. The variable is global to any subprograms of the unit that defined it. If a variable name used in the parent is redeclared by one of the nested subprograms, then inside that particular subprogram, both variables are in scope, but only the local variable is visible. The global variable can only be invoked with a qualifier. If the enclosing PL/SQL unit has no identifier, then the subprogram cannot reference the global version of the variable. A PL/SQL unit cannot access variables defined in PL/SQL units at the same level, as those variables are neither local nor global. It is also not possible to declare the same identifier twice in the same PL/SQL unit. The example below shows scope and visibility of several variables:

```
-- Outer block:
DECLARE
  v_a VARCHAR2(1) := 'A';
  v_b VARCHAR2(1) := 'B';
BEGIN
  DECLARE
    v_a VARCHAR2(1) := 'a';
    v_c VARCHAR2(1) := 'c';
  BEGIN
    DBMS_OUTPUT.PUT_LINE('Inner Block 1, variable v_a: '
                         || v_a);
    DBMS_OUTPUT.PUT_LINE('Inner Block 1, variable v_b: '
                         || v_b);
    DBMS_OUTPUT.PUT_LINE('Inner Block 1, variable v_c: '
                         || v_c);
  END;

  DECLARE
    v_d VARCHAR2(1) := 'd';
  BEGIN
    DBMS_OUTPUT.PUT_LINE('Inner Block 2, variable v_a: '
                         || v_a);
    DBMS_OUTPUT.PUT_LINE('Inner Block 2, variable v_b: '
```

```
                          || v_b);
    DBMS_OUTPUT.PUT_LINE('Inner Block 2, variable v_d: '
                          || v_d);
  END;
END;
/
```

```
Inner Block 1, variable v_a: a
Inner Block 1, variable v_b: B
Inner Block 1, variable v_c: c
Inner Block 2, variable v_a: A
Inner Block 2, variable v_b: B
Inner Block 2, variable v_d: d
```

The same block is shown again below, with the output statements removed and tags specifically noting where the scope and visibility of the v_a variable defined in the outer block changes:

```
-- Outer block:
DECLARE
 v_a VARCHAR2(1) := 'A';      <--- Scope of v_a OUTER starts
 v_b VARCHAR2(1) := 'B';
BEGIN
  DECLARE
    v_a VARCHAR2(1) := 'a'; <--- v_a OUTER not visible
    v_c VARCHAR2(1) := 'c';
  BEGIN
    NULL;
  END;                        <--- v_a OUTER visible again

  DECLARE
    v_d VARCHAR2(1) := 'd';
  BEGIN
    NULL;
  END;
END;                          <--- Scope of v_a OUTER ends
/
```

Variable v_c is not in the scope of inner block 2, nor v_d in the scope of inner block 1. If references to those variables were added to those blocks, it would generate an error on compilation, (e.g. "PLS-00201: identifier

'V_D' must be declared"). In the above example, there is no way for inner block one to reference variable v_a because the enclosing block is not named. However, in the example below, a label is given to the outer block that will allow us to access the variable by qualifying it:

```
<<outer>>
DECLARE
  v_a VARCHAR2(1) := 'A';
BEGIN
  DECLARE
    v_a VARCHAR2(1) := 'a';
  BEGIN
    DBMS_OUTPUT.PUT_LINE('Inner Block, var v_a: '
                         || v_a);
    DBMS_OUTPUT.PUT_LINE('Inner Block, var outer.v_a: '
                         || outer.v_a);
  END;
END;

Inner Block, var v_a: a
Inner Block, var outer.v_a: A
```

Write readable code with appropriate indentation

A quote that I pull out every once in a while when someone mentions that I have not made my code readable enough is: 'Code is hard to write. It should be hard to read.' It's a bad joke -- on more than one level. Generally the person hurt the most by my code when it is hard to read is me when I have to go back in and debug or make changes. If you are just starting out with PL/SQL, start out with a habit of writing clean code. If you are new to PL/SQL, it might not be good code, but make it clean code. There are four basic tenets to writing readable code:

Identifiers -- Earlier in this guide I noted the importance of using a standard naming convention for identifiers.
Whitespace -- Carriage returns in PL/SQL blocks can make related elements stand out better.
Capitalization -- A standard convention of capitalizing various words can make a big difference in the readability of code.

Indentation -- Indenting loops and control statements is critical to making the program logic more understandable. In addition, indenting elements of SQL statements in your code can make them easier to understand.

Capitalization

The test objective only deals with indentation, but capitalization is almost as important to readable code. There is, unfortunately, no single standard to capitalization in PL/SQL. PL/SQL code can be written in upper, lower, or mixed case. You'll see examples of all of these depending on the whim of the programmer who wrote it. As I mentioned earlier with naming identifiers, it doesn't really matter which convention you decide to use, so long as you pick one and use it. You should not write code that uses a lower-case 'begin' to start a block and an upper case 'END' to stop it. This is messy and it is jarring to read. All of the blocks in this guide will be written to my own personal standard, which is to capitalize all keywords, data types, and Oracle pre-defined functions and procedures (BEGIN, SELECT, VARCHAR2, DBMS_OUTPUT). All identifiers, including variables, tables (whether user-created or data dictionary tables), columns, and parameters are in lower-case. I should note that when I have been accused of not making my code readable enough, it's in reference to a lack of comments, not a lack of formatting. I will grant that I don't comment my code often enough. Luckily that isn't a test objective.

Indentation

To make the beginning and end of PL/SQL control elements more obvious, you should indent every time you start a new control element, be that a loop or a condition. The indentation can be performed with either spaces or tabs. If you nest multiple levels of control elements, the indentation should indicate what level a given set of code belongs to. The example below demonstrates indentation of a PL/SQL block:

```
DECLARE
  v_ndx1     NUMBER    := 1;
  v_ndx2     NUMBER    := 1;
  v_ndx3     NUMBER    := 5;
BEGIN
  WHILE v_ndx1 < 10 LOOP
    IF v_ndx2 > 5 THEN
      FOR v_Lp IN 1..v_ndx3 LOOP
        NULL;
      END LOOP;
    ELSE
      v_ndx2 := v_ndx2 + 1;
    END IF;
    v_ndx1 := v_ndx1 + 1;
  END LOOP;
END;
```

While the code in the example above has no point, it is at least readable. The same code below with no indentation is pointless **and** unreadable:

```
DECLARE
v_ndx1     NUMBER    := 1;
v_ndx2     NUMBER    := 1;
v_ndx3     NUMBER    := 5;
BEGIN
WHILE v_ndx1 < 10 LOOP
IF v_ndx2 > 5 THEN
FOR v_Lp IN 1..v_ndx3 LOOP
NULL;
END LOOP;
ELSE
v_ndx2 := v_ndx2 + 1;
END IF;
v_ndx1 := v_ndx1 + 1;
END LOOP;
END;
```

Providing indentation on SQL statements can likewise make all the difference between clarity and confusion. The same SQL statement is shown twice below, the first version indented and the second not.

```
DECLARE
  v_apt_name    VARCHAR2(20);
  v_apt_abbr    VARCHAR2(5);
BEGIN
  SELECT apt_name, apt_abbr
  INTO   v_apt_name, v_apt_abbr
  FROM   airports apt
         INNER JOIN aircraft_fleet afl
         ON apt.apt_id = afl.apt_id
         INNER JOIN aircraft_types act
         ON act.act_id = afl.act_id
  WHERE  afl_id IN (SELECT afl_id
                    FROM   employees
                    WHERE  emp_last IN ('Picard', 'McCoy',
                                        'Aptop')
                   );
END;
```

```
DECLARE
v_apt_name VARCHAR2(20);
v_apt_abbr VARCHAR2(5);
BEGIN
SELECT apt_name, apt_abbr
INTO v_apt_name, v_apt_abbr
FROM airports apt
INNER JOIN aircraft_fleet afl
ON apt.apt_id = afl.apt_id
INNER JOIN aircraft_types act
ON act.act_id = afl.act_id
WHERE  afl_id IN
(SELECT afl_id FROM employees
WHERE  emp_last IN ('Picard', 'McCoy', 'Aptop'));
END;
```

Interacting with the Oracle Database Server

Create PL/SQL executable blocks using DML and transaction control statements

PL/SQL has direct support for Data Manipulation Language (DML) and transaction control statements. That is to say you can execute these SQL statements directly inside a PL/SQL block. It does not have direct support for Data Definition Language (DDL) SQL statements or Data Control Language SQL statements. However, DDL and DCL statements can be executed from within PL/SQL using dynamic SQL. This will be covered later in this guide. Performing DML and transaction control operations then is simply a matter of wrapping SQL statements with a PL/SQL block. Several examples are below:

```
-- UPDATE statement
DECLARE
  v_empid     NUMBER    := 105;
BEGIN
  UPDATE hr.employees
  SET    salary = 5000
  WHERE  employee_id = v_empid;
  COMMIT;
END;

-- DELETE statement
DECLARE
  v_empid     NUMBER    := 105;
BEGIN
  DELETE FROM hr.employees
  WHERE  employee_id = v_empid;
  ROLLBACK;
END;

-- INSERT statement
BEGIN
  INSERT INTO hr.departments
  VALUES (280, 'Complaints', NULL, 1700);
  COMMIT;
END;
```

You should be aware that ending a PL/SQL block does not signal the end of a SQL transaction. A single transaction can span multiple blocks. If a PL/SQL block does not issue a COMMIT or ROLLBACK, the DML transaction is still active and uncommitted when the block completes.

Make use of the INTO clause to hold the values returned by a SQL statement

When issuing a SELECT statement from within a client tool like SQL*Plus or SQL*Developer, the application passes the query to the Oracle server and processes the results that the server returns -- generally displaying them on-screen and/or spooling to a file. The client tool will display the results of the query whether one row is returned or a million rows. By contrast, when issuing a SELECT statement from within PL/SQL, the results come back to the procedure and it must have code in place to process them. The INTO clause is used to direct the results from a query into variables when the SELECT statement will return one and only one row. If the SELECT statement returns multiple rows (or no rows), an exception will occur when using the INTO clause. A simple form of the SELECT INTO statement is:

```
SELECT select_item [, select_item ]...
INTO   variable_name [, variable_name ]...
FROM   table_name;
```

For each select_item, there must be a corresponding variable_name with a compatible data type. Alternately, the INTO clause might use a single record data type instead of a list of individual variables for each select_item. If the query will return multiple rows, you must either restrict the results using a WHERE clause so that only one is returned, or aggregate the results so that only a single row is returned. If there is a need to assign a large quantity of table data to variables, the SELECT INTO statement with the BULK COLLECT clause can be used. Bulk operations will be discussed later in this guide. The examples below show the use of the SELECT..INTO statement:

```
DECLARE
  v_bonus NUMBER;
BEGIN
  SELECT salary * 0.05
  INTO   v_bonus
  FROM   hr.employees
  WHERE employee_id = 104;

  DBMS_OUTPUT.PUT_LINE('v_bonus :' || v_bonus);
END;
```

```
v_bonus :300
```

```
DECLARE
  v_max_sal NUMBER;
BEGIN
  SELECT MAX(salary)
  INTO   v_max_sal
  FROM   hr.employees;

  DBMS_OUTPUT.PUT_LINE('v_max_sal :' || v_max_sal);
END;
```

```
v_max_sal :24000
```

```
DECLARE
  TYPE EmpRec IS RECORD (
    v_first  hr.employees.first_name%TYPE,
    v_last   hr.employees.last_name%TYPE,
    v_id     hr.employees.employee_id%TYPE);
  r_emprec EmpRec;
BEGIN
  SELECT first_name, last_name, employee_id
  INTO   r_emprec
  FROM   hr.employees
  WHERE  employee_id = 122;

  DBMS_OUTPUT.PUT_LINE ('Employee #' || r_emprec.v_id ||
                               ' = ' || r_emprec.v_first ||
                                 ' ' || r_emprec.v_last);
END;
```

```
Employee #122 = Payam Kaufling
```

Writing Control Structures

Identify the uses and types of control structures

IF-THEN-ELSE Statements

The IF statement evaluates one or more logical conditions. Based on the result of the evaluation, it either runs or skips a sequence of one or more statements. The IF statement has three basic forms:

- **IF THEN** -- Contains a single condition and a single set of actions. If the condition evaluates to true, the actions are performed. If the condition evaluates to FALSE, no action is taken.
- **IF THEN ELSE** -- Contains a single condition and two sets of actions. If the condition evaluates to true, the first set of actions is performed. If the condition evaluates to FALSE, the actions in the ELSE clause are performed.
- **IF THEN ELSIF** -- Contains two or more conditions and two or more actions. The conditions are evaluated serially. If any of the conditions is met, then the actions in that section are performed and none of the remaining conditions is evaluated. If none of the conditions evaluates to true and there is no ELSE clause, then no action is taken. If an ELSE clause exists, then the actions in the ELSE clause will be executed. Below are examples of each of the IF types:

IF-THEN

```
DECLARE
  v_value     NUMBER  := 5;
BEGIN
  IF v_value < 6 THEN
    DBMS_OUTPUT.PUT_LINE('v_value is less than 6');
  END IF;
END;

v_value is less than 6
```

IF-THEN-ELSE

```
DECLARE
  v_value     NUMBER   := 5;
BEGIN
  IF v_value < 6 THEN
    DBMS_OUTPUT.PUT_LINE('v_value is less than 6');
  ELSE
    DBMS_OUTPUT.PUT_LINE('v_value is >= 6');
  END IF;
END;

v_value is less than 6
```

IF-THEN-ELSIF

```
DECLARE
  v_value     NUMBER   := 5;
BEGIN
  IF v_value > 2 AND
     v_value < 4 THEN
    DBMS_OUTPUT.PUT_LINE('v_value is between 2 and 4');
  ELSIF v_value >= 4 AND
     v_value < 6 THEN
    DBMS_OUTPUT.PUT_LINE('v_value is between 4 and 6');
  ELSE
    DBMS_OUTPUT.PUT_LINE('v_value is >= 6');
  END IF;
END;

v_value is between 4 and 6
```

CASE statements

The CASE statement is designed to evaluate a sequence of conditions and run the corresponding statement for the first condition that evaluates to true. The CASE statement has two forms:

- **Simple** -- Evaluates a single expression and compares it to several potential values.
- **Searched** -- Evaluates multiple conditions and chooses the first one that is true.

The CASE statement is generally a better option than an IF statement when there are multiple different options and a different action is to be taken for each alternative. Examples of simple and search CASE statements are below:

Simple CASE

The selector in a simple CASE statement is an expression -- generally a single variable. It is evaluated against multiple selection values, each of which can be either a literal or an expression. The first statements for which selector_value equals selector will be executed. No further conditions will be evaluated. If no selector_value equals the selector, the CASE statement runs the else_statements if they exist. If they do not, the predefined exception CASE_NOT_FOUND will be raised. This is unlike the behavior of IF statements that will simply perform no action if conditions are not met and no ELSE clause exists.

```
DECLARE
  v_value     NUMBER   := 5;
BEGIN
  CASE v_value
    WHEN 4 THEN
      DBMS_OUTPUT.PUT_LINE('v_value = 4');
    WHEN 5 THEN
      DBMS_OUTPUT.PUT_LINE('v_value = 5');
    WHEN 6 THEN
      DBMS_OUTPUT.PUT_LINE('v_value = 6');
  END CASE;
END;

v_value = 5
```

The below example shows the result if none of the conditions evaluates to true and there is no ELSE clause:

```
DECLARE
  v_value     NUMBER   := 2;
BEGIN
  CASE v_value
    WHEN 4 THEN
      DBMS_OUTPUT.PUT_LINE('v_value = 4');
    WHEN 5 THEN
      DBMS_OUTPUT.PUT_LINE('v_value = 5');
    WHEN 6 THEN
      DBMS_OUTPUT.PUT_LINE('v_value = 6');
  END CASE;
END;

Error report:
ORA-06592: CASE not found while executing CASE statement
```

Searched CASE

The searched CASE statement is identical to the simple case in most respects. The only difference is that each of the WHEN clauses contain a logical condition to be evaluated. The first operation evaluating to true will be executed and the behavior of ELSE causes is identical to a simple CASE. The example below shows a searched case with logic matching the simple case example:

```
DECLARE
  v_value     NUMBER   := 5;
BEGIN
  CASE
    WHEN v_value = 4 THEN
      DBMS_OUTPUT.PUT_LINE('v_value = 4');
    WHEN v_value = 5 THEN
      DBMS_OUTPUT.PUT_LINE('v_value = 5');
    WHEN v_value =6 THEN
      DBMS_OUTPUT.PUT_LINE('v_value = 6');
  END CASE;
END;

v_value = 5
```

Expressions

An expression is an arbitrarily complex combination of operands and operators. The operands can be variables, constants, literals, operators, function invocations, and placeholders). The simplest expression is a single variable. The data type of an expression will be determined from the types of the operands and operators that comprise the expression. The evaluation of an expression will always generate a single value of that type. The simplest expressions, in order of increasing complexity, are:

- A single constant or variable (for example, a)
- A unary operator and its single operand (for example, -a)
- A binary operator and its two operands (for example, a+b)

An operation is either a unary operator and its single operand or a binary operator and its two operands. When an expression contains multiple operators, they are evaluated in order of operator precedence. The table below lists the operators ordered by precedence from highest to lowest. Operators with equal precedence are evaluated in no particular order. You can change the order of evaluation with the use of parentheses. When parentheses are nested, the most deeply nested operations are evaluated first.

- **exponentiation**: **
- **identity, negation**: +, -
- **multiplication, division**: *, /
- **addition, subtraction, concatenation**: +, -, ||
- **comparison**: =, <, >, <=, >=, <>, !=, ~=, ^=, IS NULL, LIKE, BETWEEN, IN
- **negation**: NOT
- **conjunction**: AND
- **inclusion**: OR

The example below shows the result of several operations:

```
DECLARE
  v_numrslt     NUMBER;
  v_charrslt    VARCHAR2(10);
BEGIN
  v_numrslt := 3**2;
  DBMS_OUTPUT.PUT_LINE('3**2 = ' || v_numrslt);
  v_numrslt := -2 + 1;
  DBMS_OUTPUT.PUT_LINE('-2 + 1 = ' || v_numrslt);
  v_charrslt := 4 || 5;
  DBMS_OUTPUT.PUT_LINE('4 || 5 = ' || v_charrslt);
  v_numrslt := 2 + 1 / 3;
  DBMS_OUTPUT.PUT_LINE('2 + 1 / 3 = ' || v_numrslt);
  v_numrslt := (2 + 1) / 3;
  DBMS_OUTPUT.PUT_LINE('(2 + 1) / 3 = ' || v_numrslt);
END;
```

```
3**2 = 9
-2 + 1 = -1
4 || 5 = 45
2 + 1 / 3 = 2.33333333333333333333333333333333
(2 + 1) / 3 = 1
```

The logical operators AND, OR, and NOT follow the logic shown in the table below. AND and OR are binary operators. NOT is a unary operator.

x	y	x AND y	x OR y	NOT x
TRUE	TRUE	TRUE	TRUE	FALSE
TRUE	FALSE	FALSE	TRUE	FALSE
TRUE	NULL	NULL	TRUE	FALSE
FALSE	TRUE	FALSE	TRUE	TRUE
FALSE	FALSE	FALSE	FALSE	TRUE
FALSE	NULL	FALSE	NULL	TRUE
NULL	TRUE	NULL	TRUE	NULL
NULL	FALSE	FALSE	NULL	NULL
NULL	NULL	NULL	NULL	NULL

Figure 1: Evaluating Logical Operators

Construct and identify loop statements

Loop statements in PL/SQL (or any programming language for that matter) run the same set of statements multiple times. Strictly speaking, you can have a loop that executes only one time, or zero times, but the construct is intended for multiple iterations. During the course of the loop, one or more values changes and as a result different operations are performed and/or the loop ends. If you have a loop where absolutely nothing changes from one iteration to the next, then by definition the loop is infinite, which is 'A Bad Thing'. It is possible to nest multiple loops. You can also use labels to identify loops, and this is recommended for nested loops to improve readability. PL/SQL provides four different types of loops:

- **Basic LOOP** -- Basic loops have no inherent start or end and require a statement to explicitly exit the loop.
- **FOR LOOP** -- FOR loops provide a defined starting and ending value for the loop endpoints.
- **Cursor FOR LOOP** -- Cursor FOR loops use rows returned by a SQL cursor to provide the loop iterations.
- **WHILE LOOP** -- WHILE loops will continue in a loop until a defined condition is not true.

There are four statements that allow you to interrupt or exit a loop. Basic loops must make use of one of the exit statements, a GOTO command (not recommended), or explicitly raise an exception in order to end the loop in a controlled fashion. The statements can also be used with the other three loop types. Each of the four can appear anywhere inside a loop, but not outside a loop.

- **EXIT** -- Will unconditionally end a loop immediately and pass control to the first statement in the block following the loop end.
- **EXIT WHEN** -- When a given condition is true, this will end a loop immediately and pass control to the first statement in the block following the loop end.

- **CONTINUE** -- Will unconditionally end the current iteration of a loop and pass control to the start of the loop for the next iteration.
- **CONTINUE WHEN** -- When a given condition is true, this will unconditionally end the current iteration of a loop and pass control to the start of the loop for the next iteration.

The basic LOOP statement has the following structure:

```
[ label ] LOOP
statements
END LOOP [ label ];
```

The example below shows the use of a basic loop and the EXIT statement:

```
DECLARE
  v_ndx   NUMBER := 1;
BEGIN
  LOOP
    DBMS_OUTPUT.PUT_LINE ('Inside loop: v_ndx = ' ||
TO_CHAR(v_ndx));
    v_ndx := v_ndx + 1;

    IF v_ndx > 3 THEN
      EXIT;
    END IF;
  END LOOP;
  DBMS_OUTPUT.PUT_LINE(' Outside loop: v_ndx = ' ||
TO_CHAR(v_ndx));
END;

Inside loop: v_ndx = 1
Inside loop: v_ndx = 2
Inside loop: v_ndx = 3
 Outside loop: v_ndx = 4
```

The example below performs the same logic using the EXIT WHEN command:

```
DECLARE
  v_ndx   NUMBER := 1;
BEGIN
  LOOP
    DBMS_OUTPUT.PUT_LINE ('Inside loop: v_ndx = ' ||
TO_CHAR(v_ndx));
    v_ndx := v_ndx + 1;

    EXIT WHEN v_ndx > 3;
  END LOOP;
  DBMS_OUTPUT.PUT_LINE(' Outside loop: v_ndx = ' ||
TO_CHAR(v_ndx));
END;

Inside loop: v_ndx = 1
Inside loop: v_ndx = 2
Inside loop: v_ndx = 3
 Outside loop: v_ndx = 4
```

The example below combines several elements. It nests two basic loops, both of which have labels. The inner loop contains a CONTINUE WHEN clause and an EXIT WHEN clause. The outer loop will increment from 1 to 7. Any time that the outer loop is an odd number, the inner loop will exit and begin the next iteration of the outer loop. When the outer loop is even, the inner loop will increment twice:

```
DECLARE
 v_ndxo    PLS_INTEGER := 0;
 v_ndxi    PLS_INTEGER;
BEGIN
  <<outer_loop>>
  LOOP
    v_ndxi := 1;
    v_ndxo := v_ndxo + 1;
    <<inner_loop>>
    LOOP
      CONTINUE outer_loop WHEN (MOD(v_ndxo, 2) = 0);
      DBMS_OUTPUT.PUT_LINE('v_ndxo: ' || TO_CHAR(v_ndxo) ||
                 ' ---  v_ndxi: ' || TO_CHAR(v_ndxi));
```

```
      v_ndxi := v_ndxi + 1;
      EXIT inner_loop WHEN v_ndxi > 2;

    END LOOP inner_loop;
    EXIT WHEN v_ndxo > 6;
  END LOOP outer_loop;
END;
```

```
v_ndxo: 1  ---  v_ndxi: 1
v_ndxo: 1  ---  v_ndxi: 2
v_ndxo: 3  ---  v_ndxi: 1
v_ndxo: 3  ---  v_ndxi: 2
v_ndxo: 5  ---  v_ndxi: 1
v_ndxo: 5  ---  v_ndxi: 2
v_ndxo: 7  ---  v_ndxi: 1
v_ndxo: 7  ---  v_ndxi: 2
```

The FOR loop executes one or more statements when a loop index is in a given range. The basic structure of a FOR loop is:

```
[ label ] FOR index IN [ REVERSE ] lower_bound..upper_bound
LOOP
statements
END LOOP [ label ];
```

When the REVERSE keyword is not present, the loop index begins at the lower bound and increments by one for each iteration until it reaches the upper bound. When the REVERSE keyword is used, the index runs from the upper bound to the lower, decrementing by 1. For PL/SQL for loops, the lower number is <u>always</u> to the left. Reversing the order of the numbers will result in a loop that never runs. The EXIT, EXIT WHEN, CONTINUE, and CONTINUE WHEN statement all have the same effect in a FOR loop as they do in a basic loop. The FOR LOOP in PL/SQL has no equivalent of a STEP clause to specify an index increment other than 1. You can get a similar result by multiplying references to the loop index by the desired increment. The example below shows several behaviors when the upper and lower bounds are changed.

```
BEGIN
  DBMS_OUTPUT.PUT_LINE ('lower_bound < upper_bound');
  FOR v_Lp IN 1..3 LOOP
    DBMS_OUTPUT.PUT_LINE (v_lp);
  END LOOP;
  DBMS_OUTPUT.PUT_LINE ('---------------------------');

  DBMS_OUTPUT.PUT_LINE ('lower_bound = upper_bound');
  FOR v_Lp IN 2..2 LOOP
    DBMS_OUTPUT.PUT_LINE (v_Lp);
  END LOOP;
  DBMS_OUTPUT.PUT_LINE ('---------------------------');

  DBMS_OUTPUT.PUT_LINE ('lower_bound > upper_bound');
  FOR v_Lp IN 3..1 LOOP
    DBMS_OUTPUT.PUT_LINE (v_Lp);
  END LOOP;
  DBMS_OUTPUT.PUT_LINE ('---------------------------');

  DBMS_OUTPUT.PUT_LINE ('lower_bound < upper_bound REVERSE');
  FOR i IN REVERSE 1..3 LOOP
    DBMS_OUTPUT.PUT_LINE (i);
  END LOOP;

END;
```

```
lower_bound < upper_bound
1
2
3
---------------------------
lower_bound = upper_bound
2
---------------------------
lower_bound > upper_bound
---------------------------
lower_bound < upper_bound REVERSE
3
2
1
```

The index value in a FOR LOOP statement is an implicitly declared INTEGER variable. The index is local to the loop and can only be accessed by statements inside the loop. The variable is read-only and cannot be altered by assignment. The index is undefined once the loop completes and can no longer be referenced. If the index has the same name as a previously declared variable, the loop index hides the other declaration from statements inside the loop. If nested loops use the same index name, references to the index will use the index of the local loop unless prefixed by a label. The lower and upper bounds of a FOR LOOP statement can be numeric literals (1), numeric variables (v_number), or numeric expressions (v_number + 1).

The WHILE LOOP statement runs one or more statements when a supplied condition is true. The basic structure of a WHILE loop is:

```
[ label ] WHILE condition LOOP
statements
END LOOP [ label ];
```

For as long as the supplied condition is true, the statements inside the loop will be executed and the condition re-evaluated. As soon as the condition is not true, the loop ends and the first statement after the WHILE LOOP will be executed. Unless one or more statements inside the loop make the condition false or null, the loop will continue indefinitely. The EXIT, EXIT WHEN, CONTINUE, and CONTINUE WHEN clauses can also be used to exit the loop. The example below demonstrates the functionality of a simple WHILE loop:

```
DECLARE
  v_assigned    BOOLEAN := FALSE;
BEGIN
  WHILE v_assigned LOOP
    DBMS_OUTPUT.PUT_LINE ('The assignment has been made.');
  END LOOP;
```

```
  WHILE NOT v_assigned LOOP
    DBMS_OUTPUT.PUT_LINE ('Unassigned.  Assigning now.');
    v_assigned := TRUE;
  END LOOP;
END;
/

Unassigned.  Assigning now.
```

Apply guidelines when using conditional control structures

There are a few guidelines that Oracle recommends when using conditional statements. First, if possible, use the ELSIF clause instead of nesting IF statements. The result will be code that is more readable. Of the two examples below, the second is obviously more readable.

```
IF condition1 THEN statement1;
  ELSE
    IF condition2 THEN
      statement2;
    ELSE
      IF condition3 THEN
        statement3;
    END IF;
  END IF;
END IF;
```

```
IF condition1 THEN
  statement1;
ELSEIF condition2 THEN
  statement2;
ELSEIF condition3 THEN
  statement3;
END IF;
```

Use BOOLEAN variables correctly. The value of a BOOLEAN expression can be assigned directly. It's not necessary to use an IF or CASE to determine the result before assigning it. Also you should avoid IF statements that use an equality operator with a BOOLEAN variable. BOOLEAN conditions should be stated as either 'IF variable THEN' or 'IF NOT variable THEN'. The first example below shows the wrong way to assign and test a BOOLEAN variable. The second example shows the first rewritten to the preferred method. The two are logically equivalent, but the second statement is clearer.

```
DECLARE
  v_var1    NUMBER    := 1;
  v_var2    NUMBER    := 2;
  v_bool    BOOLEAN;
BEGIN

  IF v_var1 > v_var2 THEN
    v_bool := TRUE;
  ELSE
    v_bool := FALSE;
  END IF;

  IF v_bool = TRUE THEN
    NULL;
  END IF;
END;
```

```
DECLARE
  v_var1    NUMBER    := 1;
  v_var2    NUMBER    := 2;
  v_bool    BOOLEAN;
BEGIN
  v_bool := v_var1 > v_var2;

  IF v_bool THEN
    NULL;
  END IF;
END;
```

Finally, when comparing a single expression against multiple values, the logic is simpler when a single CASE statement is used instead of an IF with several ELSIF clauses. Of the two examples below, the second is obviously simpler and easier to read.

```
DECLARE
  v_test     NUMBER     := 5;
BEGIN
  IF v_test = 1 THEN
    NULL;
  ELSIF v_test = 2 THEN
    NULL;
  ELSIF v_test = 3 THEN
    NULL;
  ELSIF v_test = 4 THEN
    NULL;
  ELSIF v_test = 5 THEN
    NULL;
  ELSIF v_test = 6 THEN
    NULL;
  END IF;
END;
```

```
DECLARE
  v_test     NUMBER     := 5;
BEGIN
  CASE v_test
    WHEN 1 THEN
      NULL;
    WHEN 2 THEN
      NULL;
    WHEN 3 THEN
      NULL;
    WHEN 4 THEN
      NULL;
    WHEN 5 THEN
      NULL;
    WHEN 6 THEN
      NULL;
  END CASE;
END;
```

Working with Composite Data Types

Create user-defined PL/SQL records

Record variables allow you to store multiple separate but related pieces of information in a single construct. Record variables can be created in three different fashions:

- Define a RECORD type and then declare a variable using that type.
- Use %TYPE to declare a record variable as a previously declared record variable type.
- Use %ROWTYPE to declare a record variable to match part or all of a row in a database table or view.

For a variable of a RECORD type, the initial value of each field is NULL unless an initial value is specified when the type is defined. For a record variable declared with %TYPE, each field inherits the initial value of its corresponding field in the referenced record. RECORD types defined in a PL/SQL block are local and are available only within the block. RECORD types defined in a package specification are public and can be referenced from outside the package when qualified with the package name. RECORD types cannot be created at the schema level. User-defined RECORD types are created by specifying a name and field definitions.

Fields are defined with a name and a data type. The initial value of all fields in a record is NULL by default. If the field is specified as NOT NULL, you must also specify a non-NULL initial value. The example below defines a record, assigns values to it, and then outputs the results.

```
DECLARE
  TYPE r_emprectyp IS RECORD (
            emp_id    NUMBER,
            emp_first VARCHAR2(30),
            emp_last  VARCHAR2(30)
           );

  r_emp_rec1     r_emprectyp;
  r_emp_rec2     r_emp_rec1%TYPE;
BEGIN
  r_emp_rec1.emp_id       := 103;
  r_emp_rec1.emp_first    := 'John';
  r_emp_rec1.emp_last     := 'Jones';

  r_emp_rec2.emp_id       := 104;
  r_emp_rec2.emp_first    := 'Fred';
  r_emp_rec2.emp_last     := 'Rogers';


  DBMS_OUTPUT.PUT_LINE('Employee Record 1:');
  DBMS_OUTPUT.PUT_LINE('------------------');
  DBMS_OUTPUT.PUT_LINE('emp_id:    ' || r_emp_rec1.emp_id);
  DBMS_OUTPUT.PUT_LINE('emp_first: ' || r_emp_rec1.emp_first);
  DBMS_OUTPUT.PUT_LINE('emp_last:  ' || r_emp_rec1.emp_last);
  DBMS_OUTPUT.PUT_LINE(' ');
  DBMS_OUTPUT.PUT_LINE('Employee Record 2:');
  DBMS_OUTPUT.PUT_LINE('------------------');
  DBMS_OUTPUT.PUT_LINE('emp_id:    ' || r_emp_rec2.emp_id);
  DBMS_OUTPUT.PUT_LINE('emp_first: ' || r_emp_rec2.emp_first);
  DBMS_OUTPUT.PUT_LINE('emp_last:  ' || r_emp_rec2.emp_last);

END;
```

```
Employee Record 1:
------------------
emp_id:    103
emp_first: John
emp_last:  Jones

Employee Record 2:
------------------
emp_id:    104
emp_first: Fred
emp_last:  Rogers
```

Create a record with the %ROWTYPE attribute

The %ROWTYPE attribute allows you declare a record variable that represents either a full or partial row of a database table or view. The record will contain a field for every column of the row, with the same name and data type. If the row structure of the table changes, then the structure of the record changes to match automatically.

- The record fields do not inherit the constraints of the columns. A NOT NULL column will not produce a NOT NULL field.
- The record fields do not inherit initial values of the corresponding columns. Record values will all default to NULL.

To declare a record variable against a full row of a database table or view, the syntax is: "**variable_name table_or_view_name%ROWTYPE;**". A record created in this fashion will have a field with the same name and data type of every column in the table. The following example demonstrates this:

```
DECLARE
  r_ctry_rec hr.countries%ROWTYPE;
BEGIN
  -- Assign values to fields:
  r_ctry_rec.country_id := 'US';
  r_ctry_rec.country_name := 'United States';
  r_ctry_rec.region_id := 2;

  -- Print fields:
  DBMS_OUTPUT.PUT_LINE('country_id:   ' ||
r_ctry_rec.country_id);
  DBMS_OUTPUT.PUT_LINE('country_name: ' ||
r_ctry_rec.country_name);
  DBMS_OUTPUT.PUT_LINE('region_id:    ' ||
r_ctry_rec.region_id);
END;
```

```
country_id:   US
country_name: United States
region_id:    2
```

It is also possible to declare a record variable against a partial row of a table or view. This is performed with the syntax: "**variable_name cursor%ROWTYPE;**" To use this syntax, you must assign a query to a cursor. A record declared against that cursor will have every column that the query selects with the corresponding data type. It is possible for the cursor to select every column in the table or only a subset. The cursor must be either an explicit cursor or a strong cursor variable. The following example defines an explicit cursor whose query selects a subset of columns from the HR.EMPLOYEES table. It then declares a record variable against the cursor:

```
DECLARE
  CURSOR c_emp IS
    SELECT first_name, last_name, job_id
    FROM   hr.employees;

  r_emp_jobs c_emp%ROWTYPE;
BEGIN
  r_emp_jobs.first_name := 'Fred';
  r_emp_jobs.last_name  := 'Rogers';
  r_emp_jobs.job_id     := 'IT_PROG';

  DBMS_OUTPUT.PUT_LINE (r_emp_jobs.first_name);
  DBMS_OUTPUT.PUT_LINE (r_emp_jobs.last_name);
  DBMS_OUTPUT.PUT_LINE (r_emp_jobs.job_id);
END;

Fred
Rogers
IT_PROG
```

Create an INDEX BY table and INDEX BY table of records

An index-by table is the legacy name for an associative array. On the test you might see it referred to by either name. An associative array is a set of key-value pairs, where each key is a unique index that acts as a locator for the associated value. The data type of the index value can be either a string type or PLS_INTEGER. Indexes are stored sorted by the index value rather than the order in which they are created. The sort order for character data types is determined by the initialization parameters

NLS_SORT and NLS_COMP. Associative arrays have the following characteristics:

- Are empty (but not null) until populated.
- Can hold an unspecified number of elements, which can be accessed without knowing their positions.
- Do not need disk space or network operations.
- Cannot be manipulated via DML.

Associative arrays are intended for temporary data storage. However, they can be made persistent for the life of a database session if declared in a package specification and populated in the package body. They are appropriate for relatively small lookup tables and passing collections to and from the database server. The following example creates and populates an associative array:

```
DECLARE
  TYPE t_region IS TABLE OF VARCHAR2(20)
    INDEX BY PLS_INTEGER;

  t_reg_tab  t_region;
BEGIN
  t_reg_tab(1) := 'Southwest';
  t_reg_tab(2) := 'Northwest';
  t_reg_tab(3) := 'Southeast';
  t_reg_tab(4) := 'Northeast';

  FOR v_Lp IN 1..4 LOOP
    DBMS_OUTPUT.PUT_LINE('t_reg_tab(' || v_Lp || ') is: ' ||
          t_reg_tab(v_Lp));
  END LOOP;
END;

t_reg_tab(1) is: Southwest
t_reg_tab(2) is: Northwest
t_reg_tab(3) is: Southeast
t_reg_tab(4) is: Northeast
```

An associative array never has more than two 'columns', the variable being indexed and the index value. However, you can combine a record with an associative array to tie multiple values to the same index. In this case, the array still has a variable and an index, but the record variable now contains multiple distinct values. The following example is a variant of the record example used earlier. In the initial example, two records were required to hold data for two employees. With an associative array, a single record declaration can hold multiple individual record values. In the below example, a record type is declared to hold the individual employee values. Then an associative array is declared to hold a table of that type. The record is populated and then assigned to the array.

```
DECLARE
  TYPE r_emprectyp IS RECORD (
           emp_id    NUMBER,
           emp_first VARCHAR2(30),
           emp_last  VARCHAR2(30)
          );

  r_emp_rec     r_emprectyp;

  TYPE t_emps IS TABLE OF r_emprectyp
  INDEX BY PLS_INTEGER;
  t_emp_tab     t_emps;
BEGIN
  r_emp_rec.emp_id        := 103;
  r_emp_rec.emp_first     := 'John';
  r_emp_rec.emp_last      := 'Jones';
  t_emp_tab(1)            := r_emp_rec;

  r_emp_rec.emp_id        := 104;
  r_emp_rec.emp_first     := 'Fred';
  r_emp_rec.emp_last      := 'Rogers';
  t_emp_tab(2)            := r_emp_rec;

  FOR v_Lp IN 1..2 LOOP
    DBMS_OUTPUT.PUT_LINE('Employee Record ' || v_Lp || ':');
    DBMS_OUTPUT.PUT_LINE('------------------');
    DBMS_OUTPUT.PUT_LINE('emp_id:     ' ||
t_emp_tab(v_Lp).emp_id);
    DBMS_OUTPUT.PUT_LINE('emp_first: ' ||
t_emp_tab(v_Lp).emp_first);
```

```
    DBMS_OUTPUT.PUT_LINE('emp_last:  ' ||
t_emp_tab(v_Lp).emp_last);
    DBMS_OUTPUT.PUT_LINE(' ');
  END LOOP;
END;

Employee Record 1:
------------------
emp_id:    103
emp_first: John
emp_last:  Jones

Employee Record 2:
------------------
emp_id:    104
emp_first: Fred
emp_last:  Rogers
```

Describe the differences among records, tables, and tables of records

Records -- The internal components of a record (called fields) can have different data types. A record variable is created either by defining a RECORD type and then creating a variable of that type or by using the %TYPE attribute against an existing record variable or the %ROWTYPE attribute against an existing table or view. Each field of a record variable can be accessed by its name. The syntax for accessing a record field is:

```
variable_name.field_name
```

Tables -- Tables are more properly called associative arrays and are one of three types of collections supported by PL/SQL (the other two are VARRAYs and Nested Tables). In an associative array, the internal components always have the same data type, and are called elements. You can create an associative array variable by defining a collection using the INDEX BY syntax and then creating a variable of that type or by using the %TYPE attribute against an existing variable. Associative array elements can be accessed by its unique index. The syntax for accessing an element is:

```
variable_name(index)
```

Tables of Records -- When a record is combined with an associative array, the features of the two and the means of accessing them are combined. It contains both fields and elements (the equivalent of columns and rows in a conventional database table). Both a record and an associative array must be declared. The syntax for accessing a given record field for an element is:

```
array_variable_name(index).field_name
```

Using Explicit Cursors

Distinguish between usage of implicit and explicit cursors

Cursors in PL/SQL act as pointers to a private SQL area that stores information about a specific SQL statement. The cursors defined in PL/SQL are session cursors that exist only in session memory. When the session ends, the cursors cease to exist. Cursor attributes allow you to get information about session cursors and can be referenced via procedural statements but not through SQL statements. There are two broad classes of session cursors:

- **Implicit cursor** -- Implicit cursors, also known as SQL cursors, are constructed and managed by PL/SQL. PL/SQL will automatically open an implicit cursor when a SELECT or DML statement is run from within a PL/SQL block. You can access the attributes of implicit cursors, but there is no means by which you can control them. The syntax of an implicit cursor attribute value is 'SQL' followed by the attribute name. For the attribute %FOUND, the syntax to access would be SQL%FOUND. The SQLattribute reference will always point to the most recently run SELECT or DML statement. If no statements have been run, the value of SQLattribute will be NULL.
- **Explicit cursor** -- Explicit cursors are constructed and managed by user-code. Explicit cursors are declared and defined in a block. They will have a name and be associated with a query. The rows returned by an explicit cursor can be processed by using the OPEN, FETCH and CLOSE statements. Alternately the cursor can be used in a cursor FOR LOOP statement. It is not possible to assign a value to an explicit cursor, use it in an expression, or use it as a formal subprogram parameter or host variable. Because an explicit cursor is named, it can be referenced by name and is sometimes referred to as a named cursor. The attributes of an explicit cursor are referenced by the cursor name followed by the

attribute. For a cursor called c_emps, the %FOUND attribute could be accessed via c_emps%FOUND.

Use SQL cursor attributes

The following attributes are available to both implicit and explicit cursors:

- **%ISOPEN** -- This attribute returns TRUE if the cursor is open and FALSE if not. For an implicit cursor, it will always return FALSE, because an implicit cursor closes once its associated statement runs.
- **%FOUND** -- This attribute will return NULL, TRUE or FALSE :
  - ✓ NULL: Implicit cursors will return NULL if no SELECT or DML statement has run in the session. For explicit cursors it will return NULL after the cursor has been defined but before the first FETCH occurs.
  - ✓ TRUE: If a SELECT statement returned one or more rows or a DML statement affected one or more rows.
  - ✓ FALSE: If a SQL statement ran but no rows were affected or returned.
- **%NOTFOUND** -- This is the logical opposite of the %FOUND attribute. It will return one of three values:
  - ✓ NULL: Implicit cursors will return NULL if no SELECT or DML statement has run in the session. For explicit cursors it will return NULL after the cursor has been defined but before the first FETCH occurs.
  - ✓ TRUE: If a SQL statement ran but no rows were affected or returned.
  - ✓ FALSE: if a SELECT statement returned one or more rows or a DML statement affected one or more rows.
- **%ROWCOUNT** -- The row count attribute indicates the number of rows that were affected by a SQL operation. It returns a NULL for implicit cursors if no SELECT or DML statement has run in the session. For explicit cursors it will return NULL after the cursor has been defined but before the first FETCH occurs. In all other

cases, it will return the number of rows returned by a SELECT statement or affected by a DML statement.

The following example shows the use of attributes with an implicit cursor. The %ISOPEN attribute and the %NOTFOUND attribute both return FALSE, and therefore the associated output lines do not run.

```
BEGIN
  UPDATE hr.employees
  SET    salary = salary * 1.1
  WHERE  job_id = 'IT_PROG';

  IF SQL%ISOPEN THEN
    DBMS_OUTPUT.PUT_LINE('Implicit cursor is open');
  END IF;
  IF SQL%FOUND THEN
    DBMS_OUTPUT.PUT_LINE('Implicit cursor affected one or
more rows');
  END IF;
  IF SQL%NOTFOUND THEN
    DBMS_OUTPUT.PUT_LINE('Implicit cursor affected no rows');
  END IF;
  DBMS_OUTPUT.PUT_LINE('SQL%ROWCOUNT: ' || SQL%ROWCOUNT);
  ROLLBACK;
END;

Implicit cursor affected one or more rows
SQL%ROWCOUNT: 5
```

The following example shows the use of attributes with an explicit cursor. From it you can see that the cursor is not open before the cursor for loop starts or after it ends. You can also see the affected ROWCOUNT attribute increases as the loop increments.

```
DECLARE
  CURSOR c_itp IS
    SELECT first_name, last_name
    FROM   hr.employees
    WHERE  job_id = 'IT_PROG'
    AND    salary = 4800;
BEGIN
  IF c_itp%ISOPEN THEN
    DBMS_OUTPUT.PUT_LINE('Explicit cursor is open before
loop');
  END IF;

  FOR v_Lp IN c_itp LOOP
    IF c_itp%ISOPEN THEN
      DBMS_OUTPUT.PUT_LINE('Explicit cursor is open in
loop');
    END IF;

    IF c_itp%FOUND THEN
      DBMS_OUTPUT.PUT_LINE('Explicit cursor affected one or
more rows');
    END IF;

    IF c_itp%NOTFOUND THEN
      DBMS_OUTPUT.PUT_LINE('Explicit cursor affected no
rows');
    END IF;

    DBMS_OUTPUT.PUT_LINE('c_itp%ROWCOUNT: ' ||
c_itp%ROWCOUNT);
  END LOOP;

  IF c_itp%ISOPEN THEN
    DBMS_OUTPUT.PUT_LINE('Explicit cursor is open after
loop');
  END IF;
END;

Explicit cursor is open in loop
Explicit cursor affected one or more rows
c_itp%ROWCOUNT: 1
Explicit cursor is open in loop
Explicit cursor affected one or more rows
c_itp%ROWCOUNT: 2
```

Declare and control explicit cursors

While implicit cursors require less code to implement, explicit cursors are more flexible and can provide functionality that is not possible with implicit cursors, such as accepting parameters. SELECT INTO and implicit cursor FOR LOOPs make use of implicit cursors that PL/SQL defines and manages automatically. In an explicit cursor FOR LOOP, you define an explicit cursor, but PL/SQL manages it. Only when you define an explicit cursor and use the OPEN, FETCH, and CLOSE statements do you have full control over the cursor and query result set processing. Using OPEN-FETCH-CLOSE for processing cursors is simultaneously more complicated and more flexible than the other methods. Some operations possible with this method are:

- Processing multiple cursors and result sets in parallel.
- Processing multiple rows in a single loop iteration or skipping rows.
- Processing a cursor in multiple loops.
- Declaring an explicit cursor in one PL/SQL unit but retrieving the rows from another.

Once an explicit cursor has been declared and opened, the FETCH statement allows you to retrieve the rows of the query result set. The basic syntax of a FETCH statement that returns a single row is:

```
FETCH cursor_name INTO into_clause
```

The into_clause can be a list of variables or a single record variable. Every column returned by the query, must have a corresponding type-compatible variable or field. The FETCH statement performs three operations:

- Retrieves the current row of the result set
- Stores the column values of that row into the variables or record
- Advances the cursor to the next row.

The FETCH statement is generally used inside a LOOP statement which exits when the FETCH statement runs out of rows. The %NOTFOUND attribute can be used to trigger the exit condition. PL/SQL does not raise an exception when a FETCH statement returns no rows. The example below shows an OPEN-FETCH-CLOSE operation.

```
DECLARE
  CURSOR c_emps IS
    SELECT first_name, last_name, salary
    FROM   hr.employees
    WHERE  job_id = 'IT_PROG'
    ORDER BY last_name;

  v_firstname    hr.employees.first_name%TYPE;
  v_lastname     hr.employees.last_name%TYPE;
  v_salary       hr.employees.salary%TYPE;

BEGIN
  OPEN c_emps;
  LOOP
    FETCH c_emps
    INTO  v_firstname, v_lastname, v_salary;
    EXIT WHEN c_emps%NOTFOUND;

    DBMS_OUTPUT.PUT_LINE( v_lastname || ', ' || v_firstname
||
                          ' makes ' || v_salary );
  END LOOP;
  CLOSE c_emps;
END;

Austin, David makes 4800
Ernst, Bruce makes 6000
Hunold, Alexander makes 9000
Lorentz, Diana makes 4200
Pataballa, Valli makes 4800
```

Use simple loops and cursor FOR loops to fetch data

Using a simple loop to fetch data is exactly what the prior example performs in demonstrating controlling a cursor. To demonstrate a slightly different concept, the below example will make use of the %ROWTYPE attribute rather than individual variables. This is a good bit easier then defining individual column variables – especially when there are a significant number of columns.

```
DECLARE
  CURSOR c_depts IS
    SELECT *
    FROM   hr.departments
    WHERE  manager_id > 200;

  v_depts  hr.departments%ROWTYPE;
BEGIN
  OPEN c_depts;
    LOOP
    FETCH c_depts
    INTO  v_depts;
    EXIT WHEN c_depts%NOTFOUND;

    DBMS_OUTPUT.PUT_LINE( v_depts.department_name ||
                          ' is at location ' ||
                          v_depts.location_id);
  END LOOP;
  CLOSE c_depts;
END;

Marketing is at location 1800
Human Resources is at location 2400
Public Relations is at location 2700
Accounting is at location 1700
```

Using a cursor FOR LOOP to fetch the above data requires considerably fewer statements. Unless there is some need for the flexibility possible with OPEN-FETCH-CLOSE cursor FOR LOOPs tend to be the better method.

```
DECLARE
  CURSOR c_depts IS
    SELECT *
    FROM   hr.departments
    WHERE  manager_id > 200;

BEGIN
  FOR v_Lp IN c_depts LOOP
    DBMS_OUTPUT.PUT_LINE( v_Lp.department_name ||
                          ' is at location ' ||
                          v_Lp.location_id);
  END LOOP;
END;

Marketing is at location 1800
Human Resources is at location 2400
Public Relations is at location 2700
Accounting is at location 1700
```

Declare and use cursors with parameters

The definition of explicit cursors can include parameters. When the cursors are opened, the parameter values are supplied and the SQL results customized for the supplied data. It is possible to use a formal cursor parameter anywhere in the cursor query that you can use a constant. Cursor parameters cannot be referenced outside the cursor query itself.

The example below defines a cursor with two parameters. When called, it will return only employees for a given job ID and whose hire date is greater than the number of years supplied. The code below opens the cursor with two sets of parameters and prints the results for each.

```
DECLARE
  CURSOR c_emps (p_job  VARCHAR2, p_years   NUMBER) IS
    SELECT *
    FROM   hr.employees
    WHERE  job_id = p_job
    AND    MONTHS_BETWEEN(SYSDATE, hire_date) > (p_years *
12);

  v_emps  hr.employees%ROWTYPE;
```

```
BEGIN
  OPEN c_emps('IT_PROG', 6);
    LOOP
    FETCH c_emps
    INTO  v_emps;
    EXIT WHEN c_emps%NOTFOUND;

    DBMS_OUTPUT.PUT_LINE( v_emps.first_name || ' ' ||
                          v_emps.last_name ||
                          ' was hired on ' ||
                          TO_CHAR(v_emps.hire_date, 'DD-MON-
YY'));
  END LOOP;
  CLOSE c_emps;


DBMS_OUTPUT.PUT_LINE('========================================'
);

  OPEN c_emps('FI_ACCOUNT', 5);
    LOOP
    FETCH c_emps
    INTO  v_emps;
    EXIT WHEN c_emps%NOTFOUND;

    DBMS_OUTPUT.PUT_LINE( v_emps.first_name || ' ' ||
v_emps.last_name ||
                          ' was hired on ' ||
                          TO_CHAR(v_emps.hire_date, 'DD-MON-
YY'));
  END LOOP;
  CLOSE c_emps;

END;

Alexander Hunold was hired on 03-JAN-06
David Austin was hired on 25-JUN-05
Valli Pataballa was hired on 05-FEB-06
========================================
Daniel Faviet was hired on 16-AUG-02
John Chen was hired on 28-SEP-05
Ismael Sciarra was hired on 30-SEP-05
Jose Manuel Urman was hired on 07-MAR-06
```

Lock rows with the FOR UPDATE clause

The Oracle database handles all row and table locking automatically unless specifically made to do otherwise. The standard locking behavior is designed to provide the maximum concurrency. It allows multiple users and applications to access and update the same data structures without interference or any need to coordinate with each other. If there is a requirement to have exclusive access to data during a transaction, it is possible to override the default locking behavior in PL/SQL DML operations using the following two methods:

- **LOCK TABLE** -- Explicitly locks entire tables.
- **SELECT with the FOR UPDATE clause** -- Explicitly locks specific rows of a table.

Locking a table is not a tested topic, but the SELECT FOR UPDATE operation is. When SELECT FOR UPDATE is associated with an explicit cursor, the cursor is called a FOR UPDATE cursor. A FOR UPDATE cursor locks the rows of a result set at the same time that it selects them. Using this clause, you can base an update on the existing values in the rows, because no other user can change the values before the transaction updates them. Some aspects of the FOR UPDATE operation are:

- By default, SELECT FOR UPDATE will wait until all requested row locks are acquired if one or more of the request rows are already locked by another session. The NOWAIT, WAIT, or SKIP LOCKED clause of the SELECT FOR UPDATE statement can be used to alter this behavior.
- Only a FOR UPDATE cursor can appear in the CURRENT OF clause of an UPDATE or DELETE statement.
- The rows of the result set are locked at the time you open a FOR UPDATE cursor. The rows are unlocked when you commit or roll back the transaction. Once a COMMIT or ROLLBACK occurs, you cannot fetch any more rows from the FOR UPDATE cursor.

- When SELECT FOR UPDATE queries multiple tables, it locks only rows whose columns appear in the FOR UPDATE clause.

The following example shows the use of a SELECT FOR UPDATE cursor. It selects all of the rows of the employees table using SELECT FOR UPDATE. it then loops through all of the rows and provides a 5% raise to all of the IT programmers (they deserve it):

```
DECLARE
  v_emp_id   hr.employees.employee_id%TYPE;
  v_job_id   hr.employees.job_id%TYPE;
  v_salary   hr.employees.salary%TYPE;

  CURSOR c_empsal IS
    SELECT employee_id, job_id, salary
    FROM   hr.employees FOR UPDATE;

BEGIN
  OPEN c_empsal;
  LOOP
    FETCH c_empsal
    INTO  v_emp_id, v_job_id, v_salary;

    IF v_job_id = 'IT_PROG' THEN
      UPDATE hr.employees
      SET    salary = salary * 1.05
      WHERE  employee_id = v_emp_id;
    END IF;
    EXIT WHEN c_empsal%NOTFOUND;
  END LOOP;
  CLOSE c_empsal;
END;
```

Reference the current row with the WHERE CURRENT OF clause

As mentioned in the above section, the CURRENT OF clause of an UPDATE or DELETE statement can only reference a FOR UPDATE cursor. The CURRENT OF clause is a PL/SQL extension to the WHERE clause of UPDATE

AND DELETE statements. When used, it restricts the statement to the current row of the cursor. The below example is a modification of the example in the previous section. In this example, rather than using the EMPLOYEE_ID column in the UPDATE statement, it will use the CURRENT OF clause:

```
DECLARE
  v_job_id    hr.employees.job_id%TYPE;
  v_salary    hr.employees.salary%TYPE;

  CURSOR c_empsal IS
    SELECT job_id, salary
    FROM   hr.employees FOR UPDATE;

BEGIN
  OPEN c_empsal;
  LOOP
    FETCH c_empsal
    INTO  v_job_id, v_salary;

    IF v_job_id = 'IT_PROG' THEN
      UPDATE hr.employees
      SET    salary = salary * 1.05
      WHERE  CURRENT OF c_empsal;
    END IF;
    EXIT WHEN c_empsal%NOTFOUND;
  END LOOP;
  CLOSE c_empsal;
END;
```

Handling Exceptions

Define PL/SQL exceptions

When an error is generated during compilation of a PL/SQL block, it is simply called a compile-time error. When an error occurs while a PL/SQL block is running, it is a runtime error (which is more commonly known as an exception). Exceptions can occur due to design flaws, mistakes in coding, unexpected input (which could be considered a design flaw), among other sources. Anticipating all possible exceptions is effectively impossible. However, it is possible to write very robust PL/SQL exception handlers that will prevent the program from being interrupted and optionally provide diagnostic information to help prevent a recurrence.

Any PL/SQL block, whether named, anonymous, nested, etc. can have its own exception section. This section is designed to trap exceptions and handle them in a controlled fashion. Exceptions that are not trapped cause PL/SQL programs to terminate abruptly and pass an error to the host environment. The exception section can be an extremely simple set of statements that ignore all exceptions (which is a very bad coding practice, but all too common), or a detailed block of code designed to detect and handle multiple different types of exceptions.

Recognize unhandled exceptions

If a runtime error occurs in a PL/SQL block, and there is no EXCEPTION clause in scope to take action on the error, then the result is an unhandled exception. When an exception is raised but not handled, an unhandled exception error is returned to the invoker or host environment. The outcome of the error at that point depends on the host environment. When a PL/SQL subprogram exits with an unhandled exception, any parameters passed by value to the program will retain the values that they had before the subprogram invocation. Any changes made by the PL/SQL subprogram do not get rolled back in the event of an unhandled exception. The example below shows the result of an unhandled exception:

```
DECLARE
  v_empid   NUMBER;
BEGIN
  SELECT employee_id
  INTO   v_empid
  FROM   hr.employees;
END;

Error report:
ORA-01422: exact fetch returns more than requested number of
rows
ORA-06512: at line 4
01422. 00000 -  "exact fetch returns more than requested
number of rows"
*Cause:    The number specified in exact fetch is less than
the rows returned.
*Action:   Rewrite the query or change number of rows
requested
```

Handle different types of exceptions

Pre-defined exceptions

There are a number of exceptions that are fairly common for which Oracle has created predefined exceptions. These are exceptions that have names declared globally in the package STANDARD. For these errors, the system raises the exceptions implicitly at runtime. Because they have names, it is possible to create exception handlers for them. The below example adds an EXCEPTION clause to the previous one that handles the ORA-01422 error encountered. ORA-1422 has the redefined name TOO_MANY_ROWS.

```
DECLARE
  v_empid    NUMBER;
BEGIN
  SELECT employee_id
  INTO   v_empid
  FROM   hr.employees;

EXCEPTION
  WHEN TOO_MANY_ROWS THEN
    DBMS_OUTPUT.PUT_LINE('Too many rows returned by query');
END;

Too many rows returned by query
```

A partial list of other predefined exceptions is:

- **CASE_NOT_FOUND** -- ORA-06592
- **COLLECTION_IS_NULL** -- ORA-06531
- **CURSOR_ALREADY_OPEN** -- ORA-06511
- **INVALID_CURSOR** -- ORA-01001
- **INVALID_NUMBER** -- ORA-01722
- **NO_DATA_FOUND** -- ORA-00100
- **PROGRAM_ERROR** -- ORA-06501
- **ROWTYPE_MISMATCH** -- ORA-06504
- **SUBSCRIPT_BEYOND_COUNT** -- ORA-06533
- **SUBSCRIPT_OUTSIDE_LIMIT** -- ORA-06532
- **VALUE_ERROR** -- ORA-06502

Non-predefined exceptions

Oracle has hundreds of internally defined exceptions (ORA-xxxxx errors). You can find descriptions of all of them in the Oracle Database Error Messages book. PL/SQL will raise an exception implicitly whenever one of these exceptions occurs. Only a tiny fraction of the internally defined exceptions are also predefined exceptions. An internally defined exception is an error condition in the database that Oracle has defined that will be raised when certain conditions are met. A predefined exception is a descriptive name assigned to an internally defined exception. For example: "ORA-01422" is an internally defined exception. "TOO_MANY_ROWS" is the predefined exception assigned to ORA-01422.

Sometimes when creating a PL/SQL subprogram, you may be aware that it could raise one or more internally defined exceptions that do not have predefined exceptions. In these cases, you should declare a name for them so that you can write an exception handler specifically for that exception condition. If there is no name defined for an exception, you can only handle it using a 'WHEN OTHERS' condition. To associate a name with an internally defined exception, you must do the following:

1. Declare the name in the declarative part of the appropriate block. An exception name declaration has the syntax:

   ```
   exception_name EXCEPTION;
   ```

2. Associate the declared name with the appropriate code for the internally defined exception. The syntax is:

   ```
   PRAGMA EXCEPTION_INIT (exception_name, error_code)
   ```

The following example gives the name X_SNAPSHOT_TOO_OLD to the internally defined exception ORA-01555 (Snapshot too old):

```
DECLARE
  x_snapshot_too_old    EXCEPTION;
  PRAGMA EXCEPTION_INIT(x_snapshot_too_old, -1555);
BEGIN
...
EXCEPTION
  WHEN x_snapshot_too_old THEN
...
END;
```

It's not feasible to declare names for every internally-defined exception. This means you can only explicitly handle exceptions that you expect. Unexpected internally-defined errors must be trapped through the use of the OTHERS clause. When using this, you can grab the specific error number and message. If you find that a procedure is prone to a specific internally defined error, you might declare a name for it so that you can handle it explicitly. The following example makes use of WHEN OTHERS to trap exceptions and outputs the name and error message encountered:

```
DECLARE
  v_empid   NUMBER;
BEGIN
  SELECT employee_id
  INTO   v_empid
  FROM   hr.employees;

EXCEPTION
  WHEN OTHERS THEN
    DBMS_OUTPUT.PUT_LINE('SQLCODE: ' || SQLCODE);
    DBMS_OUTPUT.PUT_LINE('SQLERRM: ' || SQLERRM);
END;
```

```
SQLCODE: -1422
SQLERRM: ORA-01422: exact fetch returns more than requested
number of rows
```

User-defined exceptions

It is also possible to create custom exceptions. User-defined exceptions are for creating and handling exceptions that are related to your own application or business logic. User-defined exceptions must be raised explicitly. They are not Oracle errors, so the runtime system will not be able to recognize when they occur. To raise an exception explicitly, it is possible to use either the RAISE statement or RAISE_APPLICATION_ERROR procedure. The RAISE statement explicitly raises an exception. When called from outside an exception handler, the exception name to be raised must be specified. When called from inside an exception handler, issuing a RAISE with no exception name will re-raise the current exception. Exceptions can be declared in the declarative part of any PL/SQL anonymous block, subprogram, or package. The declaration has the following syntax:

```
exception_name EXCEPTION;
```

In the example below, the procedure declares an exception named x_weekend_date. When a supplied date evaluates to either Saturday or Sunday, the procedure raises the exception explicitly, and handles it with an exception handler.

```
CREATE OR REPLACE PROCEDURE submit_timesheet (p_ts_date DATE)
IS
  x_weekend_date EXCEPTION;
BEGIN
  IF TO_CHAR(p_ts_date, 'DY') IN ('SAT', 'SUN') THEN
    RAISE x_weekend_date;
  END IF;

EXCEPTION
  WHEN x_weekend_date THEN
    DBMS_OUTPUT.PUT_LINE ('Cannot submit timesheet for
weekend dates.');
END;

BEGIN
  submit_timesheet ('17-JUN-12');
END;

Cannot submit timesheet for weekend dates.
```

Propagate exceptions in nested blocks and call applications

When an exception is raised in a procedure, the control goes to the exception section of that block. If the exception section handles the exception, then the block terminates and control is returned to the calling program. In order to handle errors successfully, an exception must be declared and associated with the error code.

If the PL/SQL block is nested and the exception is not trapped by an exception handler in the nested block, the exception propagates. The enclosing PL/SQL block will be passed the exception. If the exception is not trapped by the enclosing block, then it will in turn pass the exception to any block enclosing it, or to the invoker or host environment as an unhandled exception if it is not nested. The exception can propagate through any number of enclosing blocks (and likewise could be trapped at any level above the one where it occurred). Exceptions do not propagate across remote procedure calls.

If the exception is user-defined, then it can propagate beyond its scope. If a user-defined exception propagates beyond the block that declared it, then its name does not exist. When outside its scope, a user-defined exception can only be handled with an OTHERS clause.

There are three examples below, each with two levels of nesting. In each of the examples, the most deeply nested block raises an exception. The first example traps the exception in the innermost block. The second in the outermost, and the last does not trap it at all.

```
BEGIN
  DBMS_OUTPUT.PUT_LINE('Starting Block 1');
  BEGIN
    DBMS_OUTPUT.PUT_LINE('Starting Block 2');
    DECLARE
      v_empid   NUMBER;
    BEGIN
      SELECT employee_id
      INTO   v_empid
      FROM   hr.employees;
    EXCEPTION
      WHEN TOO_MANY_ROWS THEN
      DBMS_OUTPUT.PUT_LINE('Too Many Rows');
    END;
    DBMS_OUTPUT.PUT_LINE('Ending Block 2');
  END;
  DBMS_OUTPUT.PUT_LINE('Ending Block 1');
END;
```

```
Starting Block 1
Starting Block 2
Too Many Rows
Ending Block 2
Ending Block 1
```

```
BEGIN
  DBMS_OUTPUT.PUT_LINE('Starting Block 1');
  BEGIN
    DBMS_OUTPUT.PUT_LINE('Starting Block 2');
    DECLARE
      v_empid   NUMBER;
    BEGIN
      SELECT employee_id
      INTO   v_empid
      FROM   hr.employees;
    END;
    DBMS_OUTPUT.PUT_LINE('Ending Block 2');
  END;
  DBMS_OUTPUT.PUT_LINE('Ending Block 1');
EXCEPTION
  WHEN TOO_MANY_ROWS THEN
  DBMS_OUTPUT.PUT_LINE('Too Many Rows');
END;

Starting Block 1
Starting Block 2
Too Many Rows
```

```
BEGIN
  DBMS_OUTPUT.PUT_LINE('Starting Block 1');
  BEGIN
    DBMS_OUTPUT.PUT_LINE('Starting Block 2');
    DECLARE
      v_empid   NUMBER;
    BEGIN
      SELECT employee_id
      INTO   v_empid
      FROM   hr.employees;
    END;
    DBMS_OUTPUT.PUT_LINE('Ending Block 2');
  END;
  DBMS_OUTPUT.PUT_LINE('Ending Block 1');
END;

Starting Block 1
Starting Block 2
```

```
Error report:
ORA-01422: exact fetch returns more than requested number of
rows
ORA-06512: at line 8
01422. 00000 -  "exact fetch returns more than requested
number of rows"
*Cause:    The number specified in exact fetch is less than
the rows returned.
*Action:   Rewrite the query or change number of rows
requested
```

RAISE_APPLICATION_ERROR

The RAISE_APPLICATION_ERROR procedure is part of the DBMS_STANDARD package and can be invoked only from a stored subprogram or method. It is normally used to raise a user-defined exception and return the error code and message to the invoker. Prior to calling RAISE_APPLICATION_ERROR, you must have assigned an error_code to the exception using the EXCEPTION_INIT pragma:

```
PRAGMA EXCEPTION_INIT (exception_name, error_code)
```

RAISE_APPLICATION_ERROR is invoked using the following syntax:

```
RAISE_APPLICATION_ERROR (error_code, message[, {TRUE |
FALSE}]);
```

The error_code must be an integer in the range -20000..-20999. The message returned must be a character string of no more than 2048 bytes. When TRUE is specified, PL/SQL puts error_code on top of the error stack. If you specify false or leave it blank, PL/SQL replaces the error stack with error_code. In the example below, the submit_timesheet procedure is re-written to make use of RAISE_APPLICATION_ERROR to raise the error -20020 when a weekend date is passed to it. An anonymous block declares an exception named WEEKEND_TIMESHEET, and assigns the error code -20020 to it. When it calls submit_timesheet with a weekend date, the procedure returns the error code -20020 and a message. Program control is returned to the anonymous block, which handles the exception. The anonymous block then retrieves the exception error message using the SQLERRM function.

```
CREATE OR REPLACE PROCEDURE submit_timesheet (p_ts_date DATE)
IS
BEGIN
  IF TO_CHAR(p_ts_date, 'DY') IN ('SAT', 'SUN') THEN
    RAISE_APPLICATION_ERROR(-20020, 'Cannot submit timesheet
for weekend dates.');
  END IF;
END;

DECLARE
  x_weekend_date    EXCEPTION;
  PRAGMA EXCEPTION_INIT (x_weekend_date, -20020);
BEGIN
  submit_timesheet ('17-JUN-12');
EXCEPTION
  WHEN x_weekend_date THEN
  DBMS_OUTPUT.PUT_LINE(TO_CHAR(SQLERRM(-20020)));
END;

ORA-20020: Cannot submit timesheet for weekend dates.
```

Creating Procedures

Differentiate between anonymous blocks and subprograms

The primary differences between anonymous blocks and subprograms are listed below:

Anonymous Block

- Is not a named object (even if it has a label)
- Not stored in the database
- Compiled before each execution
- Cannot be invoked from other PL/SQL blocks
- Can use privileges assigned via a role
- Cannot have parameters

Subprogram

- Is a named object.
- Is stored in the data dictionary.
- Is compiled only during creation or modification.
- Can be invoked from other PL/SQL blocks, SQL (for most functions), pre-compilers and more.
- Can accept parameters.
- Can return a value when invoked.

Use a modularized and layered subprogram design

Modular coding allows you to write code that performs a given function a single time and then use it in many different places. When writing subprograms, it is best to create smaller subprograms that perform a specific function than larger blocks that perform several different functions. If you create a single subprogram that performs six different operations, then find later a need to perform only five of those -- it is not possible (or at least not without code changes) to use the code that already exists. If the first implementation had broken the operations into six separate subprograms, then reusing five of them (or four or three or two) at a later date would be easy.

You should also look for ways to modularize existing code after the initial implementation. If you find repeating code groups in your PL/SQL blocks, you should pull them out to their own subprograms. Add parameters as required and change the original code to call the new subprograms with the required parameters. Breaking your code out in this fashion makes it much easier to maintain and upgrade over time.

As far as layered subprogram design. There is a school of thought that pushes separating subprograms that contain SQL statements (Data Access Layer), from subprograms that implement business rules (Business Logic Layer). I've never seen a really good argument for that, but if you understand what those two are, you should be fine for the exam.

Identify the benefits of subprograms

It is easier to develop and maintain reliable and reusable code through the use of subprograms. They provide the following features:

Modular -- Subprograms can be used to break a program into manageable, well-defined modules.
Simpler Application Design -- The implementation details of the subprograms can be deferred until the main program has been tested. Individual subprograms can then be added and tested one step at a time.
Maintainable -- The implementation details of a subprogram can be altered without changing its invokers. Functions and procedures improve maintainability by storing a block of logic in a single location. Any future changes to the logic only occur in that location.
Packageable -- Groups of related subprograms can be stored into packages.

Reusable -- Multiple applications in different environments can use the same package subprogram or standalone subprogram.
Improved Performance -- Subprograms are compiled and stored in executable form. Stored subprograms run on the database server and therefore have the advantage of its power and proximity to the data. This reduces network traffic and improves response times.
Shareable -- Stored subprograms are cached and shared among users, which lowers memory requirements and invocation overhead.

Create a simple procedure and invoke it from an anonymous block

Subprograms can be called from anonymous blocks, but the reverse is not true. The following example creates a simple procedure called simple_procedure and calls it from an anonymous procedure (labeled 'anonymous').

```
CREATE PROCEDURE simple_procedure
IS
BEGIN
  DBMS_OUTPUT.PUT_LINE('I am but a simple procedure');
END;

<<anonymous>>
BEGIN
  simple_procedure;
END;

I am but a simple procedure
```

I should note that labeling the anonymous block in the above example was not required and served no purpose other than to amuse me. I'm easily amused.

Work with procedures

A procedure is a subprogram that performs a specific action. A procedure invocation (or call) is a statement. Procedures must be declared and defined before they can be invoked. It is possible to declare it first and then define it later in the same block, subprogram, or package. Alternately it can be declared and defined it at the same time. Equivalent terms for a procedure declaration are a procedure specification or procedure spec. Procedures can accept parameters, update parameters and generate a return value. They are not required to do any of these. Procedures cannot be used in SQL statements. For procedures (or functions) that contain parameters, they are declared after the subprogram name and before the IS keyword. There will always be two classes of parameters, which are defined as follows:

- **Formal parameters** -- Formal parameters are declared in the subprogram heading. For each formal parameter declaration, the name and data type of the parameter is specified, and (optionally) its mode and default value. Formal parameters can be referenced in the execution part of the subprogram by their declared names. When declaring a formal argument, only the data type should be specified when declaring an argument. The precision for a formal argument is not allowed. It is possible to use %TYPE for scalar arguments and %ROWTYPE for record arguments.
- **Actual Parameters** -- The actual parameters are specified when invoking the subprogram. These determine the values that are to be assigned to the formal parameters.

Corresponding actual and formal parameters must have compatible data types.

Formal parameters can be any of three modes. The mode of a formal parameter determines its behavior. There are three modes for parameters in PL/SQL and they determine the direction in which information is passed via the parameter. The three parameter modes are:

- **IN** -- This is the default parameter mode and need not be explicitly specified. It is used to pass a value to the subprogram. Formal IN parameters act like constants – they are read-only to the subprogram. At the time that the subprogram begins, the parameter value is that of either its actual parameter or the default value of the parameter declaration. Only IN parameters can be initialized to a default value. The actual parameter can be a constant, initialized variable, literal, or expression.
- **OUT** -- OUT variables must be specified in the declaration of the subprogram and are used to return a value to the invoker. The formal parameter will be initialized to the default value of its type (generally NULL). When the subprogram begins, the formal parameter has its initial value regardless of the value of the actual parameter. The subprogram should assign a value to the formal parameter. The invoking process cannot assign a value to an OUT parameter – they can only be written by the subprogram.
- **IN OUT** -- IN OUT variables must be specified in the declaration of the subprogram and are used to pass an initial value to the subprogram and return an updated value to the invoker. The formal parameter acts like an initialized variable. At the start of the subprogram, its value will be that of its actual parameter. The subprogram should update its value. Only IN OUT arguments can be both read and modified.

The basic syntax to create a procedure is:

```
CREATE [OR REPLACE] PROCEDURE procedure_name
      [(argument1  [mode1]  datatype1,
        argument2  [mode2]  datatype2,
        ...)]
IS|AS
BEGIN
  procedure_body;
END [procedure_name];
```

If the procedure already exists in the database, you must use the (otherwise optional) OR REPLACE keywords. The following example creates a procedure that calculates the age in dog years when supplied a given birth date. The procedure is then called from an anonymous block. The parameter value to be passed to the procedure may be specified using the positional or the named method. The named method must be used when not all parameters are specified or when they are not specified in the same order they are declared. The named method requires the use of the "=>" operator.

```
CREATE OR REPLACE PROCEDURE age_in_dog_years(p_birthdate
DATE)
IS
  v_dog_years     NUMBER;
BEGIN
  v_dog_years := TRUNC((SYSDATE - p_birthdate) / (365 / 7),
1);
  DBMS_OUTPUT.PUT_LINE('You are ' || v_dog_years ||
                       ' dog years old.  Happy birthday');
END;
```

In the first example below, the positional method is used. Note that the call to the procedure is a statement.

```
BEGIN
  age_in_dog_years('13-APR-1974');
END;

You are 267.4 dog years old.  Happy birthday
```

And no – April 13th, 1974 is not my birthday, my dog's birthday, or that of anyone I know. In the second example, named notation is used to call the procedure:

```
BEGIN
  age_in_dog_years(p_birthdate => '13-APR-1974');
END;

You are 267.4 dog years old.  Happy birthday
```

Alternately, the procedure could have been invoked from SQL*Plus using the EXECUTE command:

```
EXECUTE age_in_dog_years('13-APR-1974');

You are 267.4 dog years old.  Happy birthday
```

Remove a procedure

The statement to remove a procedure is DROP procedure_name. If the procedure is in a different schema, you must prefix the procedure name with the schema name followed by a dot, and have the appropriate rights.

```
DROP PROCEDURE age_in_dog_years;

procedure AGE_IN_DOG_YEARS dropped.
```

The DROP operation is a DDL command and therefore commits implicitly. It is not possible to recover a dropped object via the ROLLBACK command. Once dropped, it can only be recovered through the use of an export or media recovery.

Display a procedure's information

You can use the DESCRIBE command (abbreviated DESC) to list some information about a procedure. It will show all parameters for the procedure, the data type, whether they are IN or OUT parameters, and the default value (if any):

```
DESC age_in_dog_years
Argument Name Type In/Out Default
------------- ---- ------ -------
P_BIRTHDATE   DATE IN
```

You can also pull the line number and text for a stored procedure from the USER_SOURCE (or ALL_SOURCE or DBA_SOURCE) data dictionary views:

```
SELECT line, text
FROM   user_source
WHERE  name = 'AGE_IN_DOG_YEARS';

LINE TEXT
---- ---------------------------------------------------
   1 PROCEDURE age_in_dog_years(p_birthdate  DATE)
   2 IS
   3 v_dog_years    NUMBER;
   4 BEGIN
   5 v_dog_years := TRUNC((SYSDATE - p_birthdate) / (365 /
7), 1);
   6 DBMS_OUTPUT.PUT_LINE('You are ' || v_dog_years ||
   7 ' dog years old.  Happy birthday');
   8 END;

 8 rows selected
```

The USER_OBJECTS (or ALL_OBJECTS or DBA_OBJECTS) views can also be used to find information about a procedure. You can use these view to locate information about stored PL/SQL objects such as status (valid or invalid), type, time created, and last modification date.

Creating Functions

Differentiate between a procedure and a function

A PL/SQL function has the same basic structure as a procedure. However, a function heading must include a RETURN clause that specifies the type of data returned by the function. A procedure cannot have a return clause in the heading. In addition, a function must have a RETURN statement in the executable section of the block. A procedure can have a return statement in the execution block, but it is both optional and not recommended. Whereas procedures are invoked as a statement, functions are invoked as an expression (i.e. a variable is assigned to the return value of the function, or a value in a SQL statement is assigned the return value of the function). As a general rule, procedures are used to perform an action whereas a function is used to compute a value.

Only a function heading can include the following:

- **DETERMINISTIC option** -- Helps the optimizer avoid redundant function invocations.
- **PARALLEL_ENABLE option** -- Enables the function for parallel execution, making it safe for use in slave sessions of parallel DML evaluations.
- **PIPELINED option** -- Makes a table function pipelined, for use as a row source.
- **RESULT_CACHE option** -- Stores function results in the PL/SQL function result cache (appears only in declaration).
- **RESULT_CACHE clause** -- Stores function results in the PL/SQL function result cache (appears only in definition).

Some rules about functions include:

- Functions can usually be invoked from within a SQL statement.

- Functions cannot be invoked in SQL statements if they return a non-server data type such as BOOLEAN.
- Functions cannot be invoked in SQL statements if they modify the database.
- Functions must be executed as part of an expression in PL/SQL.
- Functions must be invoked in the form of an expression that utilizes the return value.
- When invoked via the EXECUTE command, a host variable must be used to hold the return value.
- Functions cannot be invoked within a CHECK constraint or the DEFAULT clause of the CREATE TABLE statement.
- Functions can be invoked from within other server-side or client-side functions.

DESCRIBE works for functions as well as procedures and provides information about the return value as well as the parameters:

```
DESC age_in_dog_years

Argument Name  Type   In/Out Default
-------------- ------ ------ -------
<return value> NUMBER OUT
P_BIRTHDATE    DATE   IN
```

Describe the uses of functions

The ability to accept parameter-based input, perform complex processing, and then return a result is hugely valuable in PL/SQL coding. Some specific examples are:

- Can provide additional capabilities to SELECT statements for operations too complex to perform via SQL.
- Can perform complex manipulation of character strings.
- Can be used in the SELECT list or in any of the following clauses of SQL: WHERE, HAVING, SET, VALUES, CONNECT BY, START WITH, ORDER BY, or GROUP BY.

- Pipelined functions can be used to return data via a SELECT operation as if it were an Oracle table.
- Functions used with associative arrays can be used as high-performance lookup tables.

Work with functions

Create

The basic syntax to create a function is:

```
CREATE [OR REPLACE] FUNCTION function_name
      [(argument1  [mode1]  datatype1,
        Argument2  [mode2]  datatype2,
        ...)]
RETURN datatype
IS|AS
BEGIN
  function_body;
END [function_name];
```

If the function already exists in the database, you must use the (otherwise optional) OR REPLACE keywords. Like procedures, functions use formal parameters to transfer values to and from the calling environment. OUT arguments are not typically used with functions because information the RETURN statement is used for transferring data out. Arguments for a function must be declared in the header section and precede the RETURN statement. The header section is declared after the function name and before the IS keyword. Local variables are defined after the IS keyword.

Functions must contain two RETURN statements. One RETURN statement must exist in the header section to specify the data type to be returned. Another RETURN statement must exist in the executable section to return the value. A function will successfully compile without a RETURN statement in the executable section, but will generate a run-time error if no value is returned on execution. This is also true if a RETURN statement exists in the executable section, but conditional logic prevents it from being reached.

The example below revisits the age_in_dog_years code that was used in the procedure example. This time the same logic is made into a function. Other than removing the DBMS_OUTPUT from the new function, the only significant differences to the code are the addition of 'RETURN NUMBER' to the heading and the RETURN clause in the execution section of the code.

```
CREATE FUNCTION age_in_dog_years(p_birthdate  DATE)
RETURN NUMBER
IS
  v_retval     NUMBER;
BEGIN
  v_retval := TRUNC((SYSDATE - p_birthdate) / (365 / 7), 1);
  RETURN v_retval;
END;
```

Invoke

As a function, age_in_dog_years can be called from a PL/SQL block or as part of the SELECT list of a SQL statement. If called from a PL/SQL procedure, it must be called as an assignment rather than a statement.

Called from SQL:

```
SELECT 'You are ' || age_in_dog_years('13-APR-1974') ||
       ' dog years old.  Happy birthday'
FROM   dual;

You are 267.5 dog years old.  Happy birthday
```

Called from PL/SQL:

```
DECLARE
  v_dog_years     NUMBER;
BEGIN
  v_dog_years := age_in_dog_years('13-APR-1974');

  DBMS_OUTPUT.PUT_LINE('You are ' || v_dog_years ||
                       ' dog years old.  Happy birthday');
END;

You are 267.5 dog years old.  Happy birthday
```

A function can be called via the EXECUTE command, but a bind variable must be used to hold the returned value:

```
VARIABLE v_dog_years    NUMBER
EXECUTE :v_dog_years := age_in_dog_years('13-APR-1974')

PRINT v_dog_years

V_DOG_YEARS
---
267
```

Remove

As with procedures, the DROP command is used to permanently drop a function:

```
DROP FUNCTION age_in_dog_years;

function AGE_IN_DOG_YEARS dropped.
```

The DROP operation is a DDL command and therefore commits implicitly. It is not possible to recover a dropped object via the ROLLBACK command. Once dropped, it can only be recovered through the use of an export or media recovery.

Creating Packages

Identify the benefits and the components of packages

PL/SQL packages are schema objects that allow you to group multiple procedures and functions along with any associated types, global constants, variables, cursors, and exceptions. As with named procedures and functions, packages are stored in the database in compiled form. Packages are defined in two parts, the specification and the body. The package specification declares public items that can be referenced from outside the package. Package specifications that do not contain cursors or subprograms can exist independently. Package specs with either of these must have an associated package body. The package body defines the code of public subprograms and the queries of public cursors. Any subprogram declared in the package specification must be defined in the body. The reverse is not true – subprograms can exist in the body that are not declared in the specification. The package body can also declare and define private items that cannot be referenced from outside the package. The body can also contain initialization information that declares global variables and an exception-handling part. Packages provide many advantages, including:

- **Modularity** -- By grouping related elements in named PL/SQL modules, it is possible to distribute required application functionality into logical groupings. The interfaces between packages can be made simple and well defined.
- **Easier Application Design** -- During application design, it is possible to create only the interface information for the package specifications. Package specifications can be coded and compiled without the associated bodies. Other subprograms can be created that reference the packages, and the bodies themselves can wait until you are ready to complete the application.
- **Information Hiding** -- It is possible to share the package specification, and hide the implementation details in the package body. This allows you to change the implementation details

without affecting the application interface. Users cannot develop code that depends on implementation details that might be subject to change.

- **Added Functionality** -- Public variables and cursors in a package can persist for the life of a session and be shared by all subprograms in that session.
- **Better Performance** -- A package is loaded into memory when any subprogram in it is first invoked. Subsequent invocations of other subprograms in the package use the incarnation in memory.
- **Fewer invalidations** -- When a subprogram in the body of a package is changed, the database does not recompile other subprograms that invoke it. Dependent subprograms rely only on the parameters and return value that are declared in the specification.

Create a package specification and body

The syntax for creating a package specification is:

```
CREATE [OR REPLACE] PACKAGE package_name
IS | AS
    public type and variable declarations
    subprogram specifications
END [package_name];
```

Any types, variables, constants or subprograms declared in the package specification are visible outside the package and can be invoked by other PL/SQL constructs. Procedures and functions in a package being invoked by external constructs must use the package name as a prefix. To make a procedure or function public within a package, declare the procedure header in the specification. The header for a procedure includes the procedure name and arguments. The header for a function includes the function name, arguments and return clause. Any public variables, types or constants referenced externally must likewise be prefixed.

The body of a package has a header, declaration, and an optional executable section. The executable section of a package body must be after all subprograms are declared. It is specified using the BEGIN keyword and ends with the END package_name line. Any code in this section is executed the first time the package is referenced within a session. The code will not be executed again unless the user changes sessions or the package is recompiled. Packages, unlike procedures and functions, cannot be called, parameterized, or nested.

The syntax for creating a package body is:

```
CREATE [OR REPLACE] PACKAGE BODY package_name
IS | AS
    private type and variable declarations
    subprogram bodies
END [package_name];
```

Any types, variables or constants declared in the package body are only visible inside the package. If subprograms exist in the package body that are not declared in the package specification, then they are private and can only be referenced from inside the package.

In the example below is a sample package. Once again, the age in dog years has been revisited. This time there is a bit more to the logic. The package calculates relative age when compared to several animal species based on average lifetimes. The package has a function called YEARS that performs the age calculation using a human lifespan of 70 years and an animal lifespan that is set by a second procedure called SET_LIFESPAN. The animal lifespan is stored in a private variable named l_animal and the human lifespan in a private constant named l_human. A public package variable called g_human is defined in the package specification. If set from outside the package, it will override the default lifespan for humans in the l_human constant.

```
CREATE PACKAGE age_calc
AS
  g_human         NUMBER;
  FUNCTION years(p_birthdate  DATE,
                 p_species    VARCHAR2)
  RETURN NUMBER;

  PROCEDURE set_lifespan(p_species    VARCHAR2);

END age_calc;


CREATE PACKAGE BODY age_calc
AS
  l_human     CONSTANT NUMBER     := 70;
  l_animal    NUMBER;

  FUNCTION years(p_birthdate  DATE,
                 p_species    VARCHAR2)
  RETURN NUMBER
  IS
    v_retval   NUMBER;
  BEGIN
    set_lifespan(p_species);
    v_retval := TRUNC((SYSDATE - p_birthdate) /
                      (365 / (NVL(g_human, l_human) /
l_animal)), 1);
    RETURN v_retval;

  END years;


  PROCEDURE set_lifespan(p_species    VARCHAR2)
  IS
  BEGIN
    CASE p_species
      WHEN 'Galapagos tortoise' THEN
        l_animal := 200;
      WHEN 'Carp' THEN
        l_animal := 100;
      WHEN 'Gray Whale' THEN
        l_animal := 70;
      WHEN 'Alligator' THEN
        l_animal := 50;
      WHEN 'Elephant' THEN
        l_animal := 35;
```

```
      WHEN 'Dolphin' THEN
        l_animal := 30;
      WHEN 'Snake' THEN
        l_animal := 20;
      WHEN 'Black Bear' THEN
        l_animal := 18;
      WHEN 'Tiger' THEN
        l_animal := 16;
      ELSE
        l_animal := l_human;
    END CASE;
  END set_lifespan;

END age_calc;
```

Invoke package subprograms

Since AGE_CALC.YEARS is a function, it is possible to call it from a SELECT statement. Note that the YEAR function is prefixed with the package name and a period.

```
SELECT age_calc.years('13-APR-1974','Galapagos tortoise') AS
AGE
FROM   dual;

AGE
---
13.3

SELECT age_calc.years('13-APR-1974','Dolphin') AS AGE
FROM   dual;

AGE
---
89.1
```

It can also be called from a PL/SQL block:

```
DECLARE
  v_years     NUMBER;
  v_animal    VARCHAR2(20) := 'Alligator';
BEGIN
  v_years := age_calc.years('13-APR-1974', v_animal);

  DBMS_OUTPUT.PUT_LINE('You are ' || v_years ||
                      ' ' || v_animal || ' years old.  Happy
birthday');
END;

You are 53.5 Alligator years old.  Happy birthday
```

So far we have not made use of the g_human variable. The example below is identical to the previous one except that it will specify a value for AGE_CALC.G_HUMAN. This changes the returned age from 53.5 to 61.2.:

```
DECLARE
  v_years     NUMBER;
  v_animal    VARCHAR2(20) := 'Alligator';
BEGIN
  age_calc.g_human = 80;
  v_years := age_calc.years('13-APR-1974', v_animal);

  DBMS_OUTPUT.PUT_LINE('You are ' || v_years ||
                      ' ' || v_animal || ' years old.  Happy
birthday');
END;

You are 61.2 Alligator years old.  Happy birthday
```

Remove a package

The DROP command can be used to drop a package. You can drop the package body only, or both the package body and the spec. You cannot drop **just** the package specification when a package body exists.

```
DROP PACKAGE BODY age_calc;

package body AGE_CALC dropped.


DROP PACKAGE age_calc;

package AGE_CALC dropped.
```

Display package information

The DESCRIBE command can be used with packages as well as functions and procedures. When run against a package, it will list all of the subprograms visible in the package specification along with any parameters and return value data types.

```
DESC age_calc

PROCEDURE         Argument Name  Type     IN/OUT Default
----------------- -------------- -------- ------ -------
SET_LIFESPAN      P_SPECIES      VARCHAR2 IN
YEARS (FUNCTION) <return value> NUMBER   OUT
YEARS             P_BIRTHDATE    DATE     IN
YEARS             P_SPECIES      VARCHAR2 IN
```

Working with Packages

Overload package subprograms

Subprograms in PL/SQL can be overloaded, which means that two or more subprograms have the same name, but differences in the parameters they accept. The difference in the formal parameters can be in number, order, or data type family. One example of the utility of an overloaded subprogram is the SQL function TO_CHAR. When passed a parameter that is a DATE data type, the function performs a much different operation than it does when passed a NUMBER data type.

You cannot overload the following:

- Standalone subprograms
- Subprograms whose formal parameters differ only in mode (e.g. IN, OUT, or IN/OUT).
- Subprograms whose formal parameters differ only in subtype (e.g. INTEGER and REAL are both subtypes of NUMBER).
- Functions that differ only in return value data type.

The example below defines two subprograms with the same name (difference). The procedures calculate the difference between two supplied parameter values. The first calculates the difference in days between two dates. The second calculates the numeric difference between two numbers. The PL/SQL engine determines which procedure to invoke by based on the data type of the actual parameters passed.

```
CREATE PACKAGE oca
AS
  PROCEDURE difference (p_firstval   DATE,
                        p_secondval  DATE);
  PROCEDURE difference (p_firstval   NUMBER,
                        p_secondval  NUMBER);
  PROCEDURE calc;

END oca;
```

```
CREATE OR REPLACE PACKAGE BODY oca
AS

  PROCEDURE difference (p_firstval   DATE,
                        p_secondval  DATE)
  IS
    v_retval    NUMBER;
  BEGIN
    v_retval := p_firstval - p_secondval;
    DBMS_OUTPUT.PUT_LINE('The date difference is: ' ||
                         v_retval || ' days');
  END difference;

  PROCEDURE difference (p_firstval   NUMBER,
                        p_secondval  NUMBER)
  IS
    v_retval    NUMBER;
  BEGIN
    v_retval := p_firstval - p_secondval;
    DBMS_OUTPUT.PUT_LINE('The numeric difference is: ' ||
v_retval);
  END difference;

  PROCEDURE calc
  IS
    v_date1   DATE;
    v_date2   DATE;

  BEGIN
    v_date1 := TO_DATE('21-JUN-12', 'DD-MON-YY');
    v_date2 := TO_DATE('21-MAY-12', 'DD-MON-YY');

    difference(v_date1, v_date2);
    difference(5, 3);
  END calc;
END oca;

BEGIN
  oca.calc;
END;

The date difference is: 31 days
The numeric difference is: 2
```

Use forward declarations

When a PL/SQL block contains two nested subprograms that call each other, then one of the two requires a forward declaration. It is not possible to invoke a procedure before it has been declared. If subprogram A calls subprogram B and vice versa, neither can be placed first. A forward declaration declares the subprogram, but does not define it. This allows you to declare and define the second subprogram that will call the one just declared. Finally you will define the subprogram that was declared earlier. The forward declaration and the definition must have the same subprogram heading. Forward declarations are not an issue in packages because the package specification serves to declare the subprogram. The example below demonstrates the use of forward declarations:

```
DECLARE
  v_verse    NUMBER    := 1;

  PROCEDURE tweedledum(p_param1     NUMBER);

  PROCEDURE tweedledee(p_param2     NUMBER)
  IS
  BEGIN
    CASE v_verse
      WHEN 2 THEN
        DBMS_OUTPUT.PUT_LINE('Agreed to have a battle;');
        v_verse := 3;
      WHEN 4 THEN
        DBMS_OUTPUT.PUT_LINE('Had spoiled his nice new
rattle.');
        v_verse := -99;
    END CASE;

    IF v_verse != -99 THEN
      tweedledum(v_verse);
    END IF;
  END;

  PROCEDURE tweedledum(p_param1     NUMBER)
  IS
  BEGIN
    CASE v_verse
```

```
      WHEN 1 THEN
        DBMS_OUTPUT.PUT_LINE('Tweedledum and Tweedledee');
        v_verse := 2;
      WHEN 3 THEN
        DBMS_OUTPUT.PUT_LINE('For Tweedledum said 
Tweedledee');
        v_verse := 4;
    END CASE;

    tweedledee (v_verse);
  END;

BEGIN
  tweedledum(v_verse);
END;

Tweedledum and Tweedledee
Agreed to have a battle;
For Tweedledum said Tweedledee
Had spoiled his nice new rattle.
```

Create an initialization block in a package body

The first time that a package is called by a session, the database will instantiate the package for that session. Every session that calls the package will have its own instantiation of it. Instantiation of the package involves initiation and will include all of the following actions that are applicable to the package:

- Assign initial values to public constants
- Assign initial values to public variables whose declarations specify them
- Execute the initialization part of the package body

The package initialization section is an optional component of a package body. If used, it will follow the declarative part of the package body. Typically it contains statements to initialize some or all of the package variables declared in the package. Since variables can be assigned a value at declaration, typically the initialization section is used only when the assignment logic is more complex than a simple expression. The initialization section is run only the first time a package is referenced in a session. The example below shows an initialization section used to populate two package variables:

```
CREATE PACKAGE initpkg
AS
  PROCEDURE call;
END initpkg;


CREATE PACKAGE BODY initpkg
AS
  l_invoked_by    VARCHAR2(20);
  l_invoked_on    DATE;

  PROCEDURE call
  IS
  BEGIN
    DBMS_OUTPUT.PUT_LINE('Package called by ' || l_invoked_by
||
                         ' on ' || TO_CHAR(l_invoked_on, 'DD-
MON-YYYY'));

  END call;

BEGIN  -- initialization part starts here
  SELECT user, sysdate
  INTO   l_invoked_by, l_invoked_on
  FROM dual;

END initpkg;


BEGIN
  initpkg.call;
END;

Package called by OCPGURU on 21-JUN-2012
```

Manage persistent package data states for the life of a session and use PL/SQL tables and records in packages

As mentioned in the previous section -- the first time that a package is called by a session, it is instantiated for that session. Part of that instantiation is setting the package state. Any variables, constants, and cursors that a package declares in either the specification or the body make up the package state. A package will be stateful if at least one variable, constant, or cursor is declared. If none of these are declared, the package is stateless. As of Oracle 11g Release 2 (11.2.0.2), the database treats a package as stateless if its state is constant for the life of a session. This is the case for a package whose items are all compile-time constants. See the PL/SQL Language Reference for more details. Every session that invokes a package will have an instantiation, and that instantiation will include the state for stateful packages. The package state is persistent for the life of a session with the following exceptions:

- The package is SERIALLY_REUSABLE.
- The package body is recompiled either implicitly or explicitly.
- If any instantiated package in the session is invalidated and revalidated, then all instantiated packages may lose the package state.

SERIALLY_REUSABLE packages allow for applications that manage memory better for improved scalability. Packages which are not SERIALLY_REUSABLE store their package state in the user global area (UGA) for each session. The amount of UGA memory required increases linearly with the number of sessions instantiating the package. The UGA memory used by the instantiation is not released until the end of the session. For packages which are SERIALLY_REUSABLE, the package state is stored in a small pool in the SGA and persists only for the life of a server call. Once the call is complete, the memory returns to the pool. For any subsequent server calls referencing the package, Oracle will reuse an instantiation from the pool. The instantiation is re-initialized, clearing changes made to the package state in previous server calls.

Local cursors and variables declared within subprograms in a package are not part of the package state. These are persistent only during the life of any given call to that subprogram and are undefined before or after. The following example shows the use of a PL/SQL table of records in a package. The table is declared as row of the HR.EMPLOYEES table using the %ROWTYPE attribute. A loop populates the PL/SQL table (associative array) with all of the records in the EMPLOYEES table. A second loop then displays three records from that array.

```
CREATE OR REPLACE PACKAGE emps
AS
  PROCEDURE show;
END emps;

CREATE OR REPLACE PACKAGE BODY emps
AS
    TYPE t_emps IS TABLE OF hr.employees%ROWTYPE
    INDEX BY PLS_INTEGER;
    t_emp_tab    t_emps;

  PROCEDURE show
  AS
    v_ndx     PLS_INTEGER   := 1;
  BEGIN
    FOR v_Lp IN (SELECT * FROM hr.employees) LOOP
      t_emp_tab(v_ndx) := v_Lp;
      v_ndx := v_ndx + 1;
    END LOOP;

    FOR v_Lp2 IN 5..7 LOOP
      DBMS_OUTPUT.PUT_LINE('employee_id:     ' ||
t_emp_tab(v_Lp2).employee_id);
      DBMS_OUTPUT.PUT_LINE('first_name:      ' ||
t_emp_tab(v_Lp2).first_name);
      DBMS_OUTPUT.PUT_LINE('last_name:       ' ||
t_emp_tab(v_Lp2).last_name);
      DBMS_OUTPUT.PUT_LINE(' ');
    END LOOP;
  END show;
END emps;
```

```
BEGIN
  emps.show;
END;

employee_id:     104
first_name:      Bruce
last_name:       Ernst

employee_id:     105
first_name:      David
last_name:       Austin

employee_id:     106
first_name:      Valli
last_name:       Pataballa
```

Using Oracle-Supplied Packages in Application Development

Describe how the DBMS_OUTPUT package works

The DBMS_OUTPUT package allows PL/SQL to display output for reporting or debugging purposes. In order for this command to display output in SQL*Plus, you must issue the command, SET SERVEROUTPUT ON. DBMS_OUTPUT was described earlier in this guide in the "Output messages in PL/SQL" topic. In addition, throughout this guide, the example code has been making use of the PUT_LINE procedure to provide visibility into what is happening in the code. While the PUT_LINE procedure is by far the most commonly used of those in the DBMS_OUTPUT package, there are other procedures. This section will provide more information on all of the procedures in the DBMS_OUTPUT package.

The various procedures in DBMS_OUTPUT are:

- **DISABLE** -- Disables calls to PUT, PUT_LINE, NEW_LINE, GET_LINE, and GET_LINES. It also purges the buffer of any remaining information. There is no need to call this procedure when using the SERVEROUTPUT option of SQL*Plus. The syntax is:

  ```
  DBMS_OUTPUT.DISABLE;
  ```

- **ENABLE** -- Enables calls to PUT, PUT_LINE, NEW_LINE, GET_LINE, and GET_LINES. If the DBMS_OUTPUT package is not activated then calls to these procedures are ignored. The syntax is:

  ```
  DBMS_OUTPUT.ENABLE (buffer_size IN INTEGER DEFAULT
  20000);
  ```

- **GET_LINE** -- Retrieves a single line of buffered information. The syntax is:

  ```
  DBMS_OUTPUT.GET_LINE (line OUT VARCHAR2,
  ```

```
                    status OUT INTEGER);
```

- **GET_LINES** -- Retrieves an array of lines from the buffer. This procedure is overloaded and has two alternate calls:

```
DBMS_OUTPUT.GET_LINES (lines    OUT CHARARR,
                       numlines IN OUT INTEGER);

DBMS_OUTPUT.GET_LINES (lines    OUT
DBMSOUTPUT_LINESARRAY,
                       numlines IN OUT INTEGER);
```

- **NEW_LINE** -- Puts an end-of-line marker. The GET_LINE Procedure and the GET_LINES Procedure return "lines" as delimited by "newlines". Every call to the PUT_LINE Procedure or NEW_LINE Procedure generates a line that is returned by GET_LINE(S). The syntax is:

```
DBMS_OUTPUT.NEW_LINE;
```

- **PUT** -- Places a partial line in the buffer. The syntax is:

```
DBMS_OUTPUT.PUT (item IN VARCHAR2);
```

- **PUT_LINE** -- Places a full line in the buffer (i.e. text plus a 'newline' character). The syntax is:

```
DBMS_OUTPUT.PUT_LINE (item IN VARCHAR2);
```

The PUT Procedure and PUT_LINE Procedure in the DBMS_OUTPUT package place information in a buffer. It is possible to read information from that buffer through another trigger, procedure, or package. The buffered information can be accessed by calling the GET_LINE or and GET_LINES procedures. In this fashion, you can pass messages between different subprograms in lieu of displaying them on-screen. The example below shows this. A message is placed in the buffer in the main block and then four nested subprograms retrieve the buffered text in turn and make a change before passing it back into the buffer for the next subprogram.

The message displayed at the end is the result from the PUT_LINE in the gv4 subprogram. Note that the subprograms are declared and defined in the reverse order they are called in to eliminate the need for forward declaration.

```
DECLARE
  v_msg      VARCHAR2(40);
  v_status   PLS_INTEGER;

  PROCEDURE gv4
  AS
  BEGIN
    DBMS_OUTPUT.GET_LINE(v_msg, v_status);
    v_msg := REPLACE(v_msg, ' i', ' wen');
    DBMS_OUTPUT.PUT_LINE(v_msg);
  END gv4;

  PROCEDURE gv3
  AS
  BEGIN
    DBMS_OUTPUT.GET_LINE(v_msg, v_status);
    v_msg := REPLACE(v_msg, 'ear', 'er');
    DBMS_OUTPUT.PUT_LINE(v_msg);
    gv4;
  END gv3;

  PROCEDURE gv2
  AS
  BEGIN
    DBMS_OUTPUT.GET_LINE(v_msg, v_status);
    v_msg := REPLACE(v_msg, 'apev', 'eat w');
    DBMS_OUTPUT.PUT_LINE(v_msg);
    gv3;
  END gv2;

  PROCEDURE gv1
  AS
  BEGIN
    DBMS_OUTPUT.GET_LINE(v_msg, v_status);
    v_msg := REPLACE(v_msg, 'I', 'A');
    DBMS_OUTPUT.PUT_LINE(v_msg);
    gv2;
  END gv1;
```

```
BEGIN
  DBMS_OUTPUT.PUT_LINE('I heard it through the grapevine.');
  gv1;
END;

A herd went through the great wine.
```

Use UTL_FILE to direct output to operating system files

The UTL_FILE package provides PL/SQL programs the ability to read and write from operating system files. Its I/O capabilities are similar to standard operating system stream file I/O (OPEN, GET, PUT, CLOSE) capabilities. The files and directories that are accessible to the user through UTL_FILE are controlled by several factors. The preferred method of granting access to an operating system directory for UTL_FILE is via an Oracle directory object. Directory objects can be created for any directory accessible to the Oracle server. Read and write access on the directory objects (and therefore the OS directory) can then be granted to individual database users. In the past, accessible directories for the UTL_FILE functions were specified with the initialization parameter UTL_FILE_DIR. Granting access using this method is no longer recommended. There are a number of different procedures and functions in the UTL_FILE package. Some of the more commonly used are:

- **FCLOSE** -- Closes a file
- **FCLOSE_ALL** -- Closes all open file handles
- **FCOPY** -- Copies a contiguous portion of a file to a newly created file
- **FFLUSH** -- Physically writes all pending output to a file
- **FGETATTR** -- Reads and returns the attributes of a disk file
- **FGETPOS** -- Returns the current relative offset position within a file, in bytes
- **FOPEN** -- Opens a file for input or output
- **FREMOVE** -- Deletes a disk file, assuming that you have sufficient privileges

- **FRENAME** -- Renames an existing file to a new name.
- **GET_LINE** -- Reads text from an open file
- **GET_RAW** -- Reads a RAW string value from a file and adjusts the file pointer ahead by the number of bytes read
- **IS_OPEN** --Determines if a file handle refers to an open file
- **NEW_LINE** -- Writes one or more operating system-specific line terminators to a file
- **PUT** -- Writes a string to a file
- **PUT_LINE** -- Writes a line to a file and appends an operating system-specific line terminator

The procedure for reading and writing to files is very similar.

1. Use FOPEN to grab a handle for a file in either Read, Write, or Append mode.
2. Use GET_LINE to read, or PUT_LINE to write to the file.
3. Use FCLOSE to close the file after all lines are read/written.

Some of the named exceptions for UTL_FILE include:

- **INVALID_PATH** -- File location is invalid.
- **INVALID_FILEHANDLE** -- File handle is invalid.
- **INVALID_OPERATION** -- File could not be opened or operated on as requested.
- **READ_ERROR** -- Destination buffer too small, or operating system error occurred during the read operation
- **WRITE_ERROR** -- Operating system error occurred during the write operation.
- **INTERNAL_ERROR** -- Unspecified PL/SQL error
- **FILE_OPEN** -- The requested operation failed because the file is open.
- **INVALID_FILENAME** -- The filename parameter is invalid.

- **ACCESS_DENIED** -- Permission to access to the file location is denied.
- **DELETE_FAILED** -- The requested file delete operation failed.
- **RENAME_FAILED** -- The requested file rename operation failed.

The example below opens a file in write mode, writes a line to it and then closes it. It then re-opens the file in read mode, pulls the line from it, and closes it again.

```
DECLARE
  v_read_data VARCHAR2(32767);
  f_fh        UTL_FILE.FILE_TYPE;
BEGIN
  f_fh := UTL_FILE.FOPEN('C_TEMP', 'utl_file.tmp', 'W');
  UTL_FILE.PUT_LINE(f_fh, 'The quick brown fox jumped over
the lazy dog.');
  UTL_FILE.FCLOSE(f_fh);

  f_fh := UTL_FILE.FOPEN('C_TEMP', 'utl_file.tmp', 'R');

  UTL_FILE.GET_LINE(f_fh, v_read_data, 32767);
  UTL_FILE.FCLOSE(f_fh);

  DBMS_OUTPUT.PUT_LINE(v_read_data);
END;

The quick brown fox jumped over the lazy dog.
```

Describe the main features of UTL_MAIL

The UTL_MAIL package allows you to send email from within PL/SQL. The package includes commonly used email features, such as attachments, CC, and BCC. In order for UTL_MAIL to be utilized, the initialization parameter SMTP_OUT_SERVER must be specified. UTL_MAIL is not installed by default because of security considerations and the initialization parameter requirement. In order to use the UTL_MAIL package, the invoking user will need to have the connect privilege granted in the access control list for the network host to which he wants to connect.

To install UTL_MAIL, you must run two scripts:

```
$ORACLE_HOME/rdbms/admin/utlmail.sql
$ORACLE_HOME/rdbms/admin/prvtmail.plb
```

The UTL_MAIL package includes the following procedures:

- **SEND** -- Packages an email message into the appropriate format, locates SMTP information, and delivers the message to the SMTP server for forwarding to the recipients.
- **SEND_ATTACH_RAW** -- The SEND Procedure overloaded for RAW attachments.
- **SEND_ATTACH_VARCHAR2** -- The SEND Procedure overloaded for VARCHAR2 attachments.

Using Dynamic SQL

Describe the execution flow of SQL statements

There are four stages to a SQL statement. Not all SQL statements will use all four.

- **Parse** -- Every SQL statement must be parsed. Parsing the statement checks the statement's syntax and associates it with the cursor (either implicit or explicit). It also verifies the existence of the objects referenced and that the correct privileges exist to process the SQL.
- **Bind** -- For SQL statements that contain input data to be supplied at runtime, placeholders in the SQL statement mark where data must be supplied. For each placeholder, values must be supplied to complete the SQL statement. When the statement is run, Oracle binds these variables to the operation. The bind step only occurs when a SQL statement contains one or more bind variables.
- **Execute** -- The server executes the statement at this point. For any SQL operation except SELECT, this is the last step.
- **Fetch** -- The fetch operation retrieves the rows that satisfy the query. The fetch operation will continue until all the rows of the query have been returned.

Use Native Dynamic SQL (NDS)

While it is possible to run static SQL statements directly from within PL/SQL, there are limitations to what can be done in this fashion. In these cases making use of dynamic SQL is required. Dynamic SQL statements are not embedded in the PL/SQL source code. Instead, they are stored or constructed character strings that are executed as SQL by the program at runtime. The ability to dynamically change the SQL to be executed at runtime enables you to create more flexible procedures. Dynamic SQL allows you to perform tasks such as selecting from a table whose name is not known until runtime. Dynamic SQL is required in the following cases:

- SQL for which the text is unknown at compile time.
- When there is a need to perform DDL and DCL operations.
- When compilation creates schema object dependencies.

The vast majority of the cases where static SQL is not applicable can be satisfied using Native Dynamic SQL (NDS). NDS can handle most dynamic SQL statements using the EXECUTE IMMEDIATE statement. If the SQL statement is self-contained, requiring no bind variables and returning no results, then the EXECUTE IMMEDIATE statement needs no clauses. If the statement requires bind variables, each placeholder must have a corresponding bind variable in the appropriate clause of the EXECUTE IMMEDIATE statement.

For SELECT statements that return multiple rows, NDS gives you these choices:

- The EXECUTE IMMEDIATE can be used with the BULK COLLECT INTO clause.
- The OPEN FOR, FETCH, and CLOSE statements can be used in lieu of EXECUTE IMMEDIATE.

EXECUTE IMMEDIATE has these clauses:

- **INTO** -- Used to designate variables to hold the results of a SELECT statement that returns a single row
- **BULK COLLECT INTO** -- Used to designate variables to hold the results of a SELECT statement that returns multiple rows.
- **USING** -- Allows you to designate incoming or outgoing bind arguments to the dynamic SQL.

The syntax for EXECUTE IMMEDIATE IS:

```
EXECUTE IMMEDIATE sql_statement
[INTO  {variable
      [,variable] ... record}]
[USING   [IN|OUT|IN OUT] bind_argument
      [, [IN|OUT|IN OUT] bind_argument] ... ];
```

The below example uses NDS to construct a SQL statement that dynamically sets the value to filter the EMPLOYEES table by **and** the column to be used. Because the EXECUTE IMMEDIATE uses the INTO clause, it will fail with an error if more than one row is returned.

```
CREATE PROCEDURE get_employee(p_column   VARCHAR2,
                              p_value    VARCHAR2)
IS
  v_SQL     VARCHAR2(200);
  v_row     hr.employees%ROWTYPE;
BEGIN
  v_SQL := 'SELECT * FROM hr.employees WHERE ' ||
           p_column || ' = ''' || p_value || '''';

  EXECUTE IMMEDIATE v_SQL INTO v_row;

  DBMS_OUTPUT.PUT_LINE('Employee is ' || v_row.first_name ||
                       ' ' || v_row.last_name);
END;

BEGIN
  get_employee('employee_id', '101');
  get_employee('last_name', 'Ernst');
  get_employee('phone_number', '515.124.4369');
END;

Employee is Neena Kochhar
Employee is Bruce Ernst
Employee is Ismael Sciarra
```

The following example uses EXECUTE IMMEDIATE with BULK COLLECT in order to handle a multi-row query. In order to use the BULK COLLECT option, a TABLE must be declared to hold the retrieved values. Each row of the query is referenced by the index value of the order in which it was fetched.

```
DECLARE
  TYPE t_emp_tab IS TABLE OF hr.employees%ROWTYPE;

  t_tab     t_emp_tab;
BEGIN
  EXECUTE IMMEDIATE 'SELECT * FROM hr.employees'
  BULK COLLECT INTO t_tab;

  DBMS_OUTPUT.PUT_LINE('First row: ' || t_tab(1).first_name
||
                        ' ' || t_tab(1).last_name);
  DBMS_OUTPUT.PUT_LINE('Second row: ' || t_tab(2).first_name
||
                        ' ' || t_tab(2).last_name);
  DBMS_OUTPUT.PUT_LINE('Third row: ' || t_tab(3).first_name
||
                        ' ' || t_tab(3).last_name);
END;

First row: Steven King
Second row: Neena Kochhar
Third row: Lex De Haan
```

The following example demonstrates the same functionality using OPEN-FETCH-CLOSE instead of the EXECUTE IMMEDIATE statement. The OPEN-FETCH-CLOSE can also be used without BULK COLLECT by performing the FETCH in a loop.

```
DECLARE
  TYPE t_emp_tab IS TABLE OF hr.employees%ROWTYPE;

  t_tab     t_emp_tab;
  c_emps    SYS_REFCURSOR;
BEGIN
  OPEN  c_emps FOR 'SELECT * FROM hr.employees';
  FETCH c_emps
  BULK COLLECT INTO t_tab;
  CLOSE c_emps;
```

```
  DBMS_OUTPUT.PUT_LINE('First row: ' || t_tab(1).first_name
                       || ' ' || t_tab(1).last_name);
  DBMS_OUTPUT.PUT_LINE('Second row: ' || t_tab(2).first_name
                       || ' ' || t_tab(2).last_name);
  DBMS_OUTPUT.PUT_LINE('Third row: ' || t_tab(3).first_name
                       || ' ' || t_tab(3).last_name);
END;

First row: Steven King
Second row: Neena Kochhar
Third row: Lex De Haan
```

Use the DBMS_SQL package

The DBMS_SQL package can also be used to generate dynamic SQL in PL/SQL. In most situations, NDS is easier to implement and performs better than DBMS_SQL. However, there are limitations to Native Dynamic SQL that sometimes require the use of DBMS SQL. In particular, there is no support in NDS for dynamic SQL statements that have an unknown number of inputs or outputs. In addition, there are some tasks that can only be performed using DBMS_SQL. The DBMS_SQL package is owned by the SYS schema and compiled with AUTHID CURRENT_USER. This means subprograms in the package that are called from an anonymous PL/SQL block are run using the privileges of the current user.

In certain situations, you must use native dynamic SQL instead of the DBMS_SQL package:

- The dynamic SQL statement needs to retrieves rows into records.
- There is a need to use the SQL cursor attribute %FOUND, %ISOPEN, %NOTFOUND, or %ROWCOUNT after issuing a dynamic SQL statement that is an INSERT, UPDATE, DELETE, or single-row SELECT statement.

When you need both the DBMS_SQL package and native dynamic SQL, the following two functions allow you to switch between them:

- **DBMS_SQL.TO_REFCURSOR** -- Converts a SQL cursor number to a weak cursor variable, which you can use in native dynamic SQL statements.
- **DBMS_SQL.TO_CURSOR_NUMBER** -- Converts a REF CURSOR variable (either strong or weak) to a SQL cursor number, which you can pass to DBMS_SQL subprograms.

The example below demonstrates the use of the DBMS_SQL package to perform a SELECT statement with bind variables. When compared to what would be required with EXECUTE IMMEDIATE, it's clear why no one uses DBMS_SQL except in cases where it is necessary.

```
CREATE PROCEDURE emps_ds(p_empid
hr.employees.employee_id%TYPE)
AS

  v_cursor     PLS_INTEGER;
  v_emp_first  VARCHAR2(20);
  v_emp_last   VARCHAR2(20);
  v_rows       PLS_INTEGER;
BEGIN
  v_cursor := DBMS_SQL.OPEN_CURSOR;
  DBMS_SQL.PARSE(v_cursor, 'SELECT first_name, last_name ' ||
                           'FROM   hr.employees ' ||
                           'WHERE  employee_id < :x',
DBMS_SQL.NATIVE);
  DBMS_SQL.BIND_VARIABLE(v_cursor, ':x', p_empid);
  DBMS_SQL.DEFINE_COLUMN(v_cursor, 1, v_emp_first, 20);
  DBMS_SQL.DEFINE_COLUMN(v_cursor, 2, v_emp_last, 20);
  v_rows := DBMS_SQL.EXECUTE(v_cursor);

  LOOP
    IF DBMS_SQL.FETCH_ROWS(v_cursor) = 0 then
       EXIT;
    END IF;
    DBMS_SQL.COLUMN_VALUE(v_cursor, 1, v_emp_first);
    DBMS_SQL.COLUMN_VALUE(v_cursor, 2, v_emp_last);
    DBMS_OUTPUT.PUT_LINE('Employee name: ' || v_emp_first ||
                                         ' ' || v_emp_last);
  END LOOP;
  DBMS_SQL.CLOSE_CURSOR(v_cursor);
```

```
EXCEPTION
  WHEN OTHERS THEN
       DBMS_SQL.CLOSE_CURSOR(v_cursor);
END;

Employee name: Steven King
Employee name: Neena Kochhar
Employee name: Lex De Haan
Employee name: Alexander Hunold
```

Design Considerations for PL/SQL Code

Create standard constants and exceptions

Standardizing constants and exceptions is generally performed by declaring them in a dedicated package specification (i.e. one with no accompanying package body). This allows the use of a consistent set of constants and exceptions to be used across all of the code implemented on that database. If there are any changes to these values, then they need be made in only a single location, considerably simplifying maintenance requirements.

```
CREATE PACKAGE std_names
AS
  c_domain       CONSTANT VARCHAR2(100) := 'thiscompany.com';
  c_serverip     CONSTANT VARCHAR2(20)  := '10.10.10.10';
  c_smtp_server CONSTANT VARCHAR2(20)  := '10.10.10.11';
  c_err_notice   CONSTANT VARCHAR2(100) := 'dba@' || c_domain;

  x_snapshot_too_old    EXCEPTION;
  PRAGMA EXCEPTION_INIT(x_snapshot_too_old, -1555);

END std_names;
```

The code below looks for the defined exception X_SNAPSHOT_TOO_OLD and sends email to the address defined in the STD_NAMES package specification as the destination for error notices:

```
PROCEDURE anyproc
AS
BEGIN
...
EXCEPTION
  WHEN std_names.x_snapshot_too_old THEN
    email_pkg.send_mail(std_names.c_err_notice, 'Error in
anyproc: ' || SQLERRM);
END anyproc;
```

Write and call local subprograms

A local subprogram (also called a nested subprogram) is created within the declaration section of a PL/SQL block. It is accessible only to the block in which it is declared. Local subprograms can be used when there is a given set of code that must be performed multiple times within a block, but has no utility outside that block. If the code might ever need to be executed from outside the procedure, then the subprogram should be written as a packaged or stand-alone procedure instead. Used properly, local subprograms can both shrink the size of the block and simplify maintenance. Local subprograms must be declared at the end of the declarative section after all local variables. The example below shows the use of a local subprogram:

```
CREATE PROCEDURE emp_years(p_emp_id   NUMBER)
AS
  v_row    hr.employees%ROWTYPE;

  FUNCTION yrs_employed(p_hiredate   DATE)
  RETURN NUMBER
  AS
  BEGIN
    RETURN TRUNC((SYSDATE - p_hiredate)/365);
  END yrs_employed;
BEGIN
  SELECT *
  INTO   v_row
  FROM   hr.employees
  WHERE  employee_id = p_emp_id;

  DBMS_OUTPUT.PUT_LINE(v_row.first_name || ' ' ||
                       v_row.last_name || ': ' ||
                       yrs_employed(v_row.hire_date) ||
                       ' years.');
END emp_years;

BEGIN
  emp_years(106);
END;

Valli Pataballa: 6 years.
```

Control the run-time privileges of a subprogram

Subprograms execute with the privileges of their owner, by default. This allows indirect access to database objects and more granular data security. Users only need to be granted the privilege to execute the procedure and not on the objects accessed by the subprogram. The AUTHID property of a stored PL/SQL unit determines the authorization under which a PL/SQL subprogram operates at run-time. This affects the name resolution and privilege checking when it issues SQL statements. The AUTHID property has no effect on compilation of the subprogram. For stored PL/SQL units that you create with the following statements, you can use the clause to specify either DEFINER (the default) or CURRENT_USER:

- **CREATE FUNCTION name RETURN type AUTHID CURRENT_USER...**
- **CREATE PACKAGE name AUTHID CURRENT_USER...**
- **CREATE PROCEDURE name AUTHID CURRENT_USER...**
- **CREATE TYPE name AUTHID CURRENT_USER...**

The two options for authorization are:

- **CURRENT_USER** -- When AUTHID is set to CURRENT_USER, the unit is called an invoker's rights unit, or IR unit. When the PL/SQL subprogram is executed, it will run using the rights of the person that invoked the code, not the person who created it.
- **DEFINER** -- When AUTHID is set to DEFINER, the unit is called a definer's rights unit, or DR unit. When the PL/SQL subprogram is executed, it will run using the rights of the person that created the code, not the person who invoked it. A trigger or view always behaves like a DR unit.

Perform autonomous transactions

Autonomous transactions are transactions which are initiated from another transaction (the main transaction) but which are independent of it. SQL operations performed by the autonomous transactions are committed or rolled back without impacting the main transaction. While an autonomous transaction is started by a main transaction, it is not considered a nested transaction for the following reasons:

- The two transactions do not share transactional resources (such as locks).
- It does not depend on the main transaction.
- Changes committed in the autonomous transaction are visible to other transactions before the main transaction commits.

If an autonomous transaction causes an exception, only the changes from it are rolled back. The main transaction is unaffected. To declare an autonomous transaction, use the AUTONOMOUS_TRANSACTION pragma. The AUTONOMOUS_TRANSACTION pragma cannot be set to an entire package or ADT, but it could be added to every subprogram in a package or each method of an ADT. Changes made by an autonomous transaction are visible to immediately when it commits. If the main transaction has its isolation level set to READ COMMITTED (the default), the changes will be visible when it resumes. However, it the isolation level is set to SERIALIZABLE, the changes are not visible to the main transaction when it resumes. The syntax for setting the isolation level is:

```
SET TRANSACTION ISOLATION LEVEL SERIALIZABLE;
```

The first SQL statement in an autonomous routine begins an autonomous transaction. If that transaction is ended and another one is started in the same subprogram, the next SQL statement begins a new autonomous transaction. Autonomous transactions are controlled using the same transaction control statements as normal transactions. However, they apply only to the current (active) transaction:

- **COMMIT**
- **ROLLBACK [TO savepoint_name]**
- **SAVEPOINT savepoint_name**
- **SET TRANSACTION**

Once program control is in the executable section of an autonomous routine, the main transaction is suspended. The main transaction resumes once the autonomous routine ends. Attempting to exit an active autonomous transaction without committing or rolling back will generate an exception. To exit normally, all autonomous transactions <u>must</u> be explicitly committed or rolled back.

```
CREATE PROCEDURE eoy_bonus (p_emp_id   NUMBER,
                            p_amount   NUMBER)
AS
PRAGMA AUTONOMOUS_TRANSACTION;
BEGIN
  UPDATE hr.employees
  SET    salary = salary + p_amount
  WHERE  employee_id = p_emp_id;
  COMMIT;
END eoy_bonus;
```

Use NOCOPY hint, PARALLEL ENABLE hint and DETERMINISTIC clause

NOCOPY

For subprograms that have parameters, the formal parameters are declared in the subprogram heading. The formal parameter declaration specifies the name and data type of the parameter. Optionally it might declare a mode and default value. When the subprogram is invoked, you specify the actual parameters whose values are to be assigned to the formal parameters. The NOCOPY hint exists because of the fact that formal and actual parameters are not the same thing. There are three parameter modes in PL/SQL: IN, OUT, and IN/OUT. When a formal parameter is of mode IN, the actual parameter passed to it will never change when the subprogram is invoked. However, for formal parameters of the OUT or IN/OUT modes, the value of the actual parameter can (and usually will) change. When the PL/SQL compiler passes an actual parameter by reference, the actual and formal parameters refer to the same memory location. Therefore, if the subprogram changes the value of the formal parameter, the change shows immediately in the actual parameter.

IN parameters are always passed by reference. This can never cause a problem because the value of IN parameters cannot be changed by the subprogram. OUT and IN/OUT parameters are normally passed by value. This will mean that the formal and actual parameters are using different memory locations. This is slower than passing by reference. In cases where the parameters are large data structures such as a collection, passing by reference rather than by value could represent a significant performance enhancement. NOCOPY **asks** the compiler to pass the corresponding actual parameter by reference instead of by value. Whenever the subprogram is invoked, the optimizer decides, silently, whether to obey or disregard NOCOPY.

PARALLEL_ENABLE

Including the PARALLEL_ENABLE keyword when a function is created allows it to be executed in parallel. It indicates that the function is safe for use in slave sessions of parallel DML evaluations. A function created with this keyword must not use session state, such as package variables, as they might not be shared among the parallel execution servers. PARALLEL_ENABLE also cannot be specified for nested functions.

DETERMINISTIC

The DETERMINISTIC keyword tells the optimizer that given a certain set of parameters, the function will always returns the same value. Specifying DETERMINISTIC for functions where this is not true will generate unreliable results. For functions created with this clause, if a function is called with parameters that have been used previously, the optimizer can use the previous result instead of invoking the function code again. Depending on the amount of code involved, this might produce much faster results and reduced overhead.

These semantic rules govern its use:

- You can declare a schema-level subprogram DETERMINISTIC.
- You can declare a package-level subprogram DETERMINISTIC in the package specification but not in the package body.
- You cannot declare DETERMINISTIC a private subprogram.
- A DETERMINISTIC subprogram can invoke another subprogram whether the called program is declared DETERMINISTIC or not.

Use bulk binding and the RETURNING clause with DML

The Oracle database has a SQL engine and a PL/SQL engine. The two communicate very well, but they each do their own job. Whenever SQL is executed from a PL/SQL procedure, the PL/SQL engine sends the query or DML statement to the SQL engine. The SQL engine runs the query or DML statement and returns the result to the PL/SQL engine. Bulk SQL minimizes the communication overhead between the two in order to improve performance. The BULK COLLECT clause returns results from SQL to PL/SQL in batches rather than one at a time. The larger the number of rows affected by a SQL operation, the larger the performance improvement that bulk SQL is likely to provide. A query that uses bulk SQL can return any number of rows, without requiring individual FETCH statements. Using the BULK COLLECT clause, the entire result set can be retrieved and stored in one or more collection variables in a single operation (memory permitting). For operations involving huge numbers of rows, the bulk operations are often done in chunks (i.e. 100,000 rows at a time). This is considerably more efficient than retrieving one result row at a time in a loop operation. The BULK COLLECT clause can appear in the following locations:

- SELECT INTO statement
- FETCH statement
- RETURNING INTO clause of DELETE, INSERT, UPDATE, and EXECUTE IMMEDIATE statements

The below example uses BULK COLLECT to populate two variables with all of the first and last names from the HR.EMPLOYEES table and then outputs the variable data for the first three rows.

```
DECLARE
  TYPE t_firstTyp IS TABLE OF hr.employees.first_name%TYPE;
  TYPE t_lastTyp IS TABLE OF hr.employees.last_name%TYPE;

  t_first      t_firstTyp;
  t_last       t_lastTyp;
BEGIN
  SELECT first_name, last_name
  BULK COLLECT INTO t_first, t_last
  FROM  hr.employees
  ORDER BY employee_id;

  FOR v_Lp IN 1 .. 3 LOOP
    DBMS_OUTPUT.PUT_LINE (t_first(v_Lp) || ' ' ||
t_last(v_Lp));
  END LOOP;
END;

Steven King
Neena Kochhar
Lex De Haan
```

FORALL Statement

Another feature of bulk SQL is the FORALL statement. The BULK COLLECT operation gathers the results from a SQL SELECT operation in batches rather than one row at a time. The FORALL operation sends DML statements from PL/SQL to SQL in batches rather than one at a time. A FORALL statement is usually much faster that performing the same operation one row at a time in a FOR LOOP. However, it is less flexible. Multiple DML statements can be issued in a PL/SQL LOOP, while a FORALL statement can contain only one. When sending a batch of DML statements through FORALL, they will differ only in their VALUES and WHERE clauses. The values for those clauses must come from populated collections. The first example below inserts a set of collection elements into a table using a FOR LOOP. The second set of code performs the same operation using the FORALL statement. In both cases, the code will be deleting employee records for five different job codes.

```
DROP TABLE temp_emp;
CREATE TABLE temp_emp AS SELECT * FROM hr.employees;

DECLARE
  TYPE     t_JobArray IS VARRAY(20) OF VARCHAR2(10);
  v_jobs   t_JobArray := t_JobArray('MK_MAN', 'MK_REP',
                         'PR_REP', 'SA_MAN', 'SA_REP');
BEGIN
  FOR v_Lp IN v_jobs.FIRST..v_jobs.LAST LOOP
    DELETE FROM temp_emp
    WHERE  job_id = v_jobs(v_Lp);
  END LOOP;
END;


DROP TABLE temp_emp;
CREATE TABLE temp_emp AS SELECT * FROM hr.employees;
```

```
DECLARE
  TYPE      t_JobArray IS VARRAY(20) OF VARCHAR2(10);
  v_jobs    t_JobArray := t_JobArray('MK_MAN', 'MK_REP',
                             'PR_REP', 'SA_MAN', 'SA_REP');
BEGIN
  FORALL v_Lp IN v_jobs.FIRST..v_jobs.LAST
    DELETE FROM temp_emp
    WHERE  job_id = v_jobs(v_Lp);
END;
```

The real benefit of using the FORALL statement is the reduction of context switching. In the FOR LOOP block, the LOOP itself is a PL/SQL operation and is handled by the PL/SQL engine. The DELETE statement is a SQL operation and is handled by the SQL engine. When the PL/SQL block gets to the DELETE, the operation stops being handled by the PL/SQL engine and control is passed to the SQL engine (this is called a context switch). Once the DELETE is complete and the block gets to the 'END LOOP' line, control is handed back to the PL/SQL engine (requiring another context switch). The block loops back to the DELETE and the process is repeated. Since there are five job codes in the example, there are ten context switches. In the second example, the FORALL acts to supply information for the DELETEs to the SQL engine without requiring context switches. Once control passes to the DELETE statement, the SQL engine retains control for all five operations, only returning to the PL/SQL engine at the end. When thousands of rows are affected, the FORALL statement can produce markedly faster results than an equivalent FOR LOOP.

RETURNING INTO

The RETURNING INTO clause can appear in an INSERT, UPDATE, DELETE, or EXECUTE IMMEDIATE statement when used with the BULK COLLECT clause. The RETURNING INTO clause specifies variables in which to store returned values. They can be either individual variables or collections. For statements that affect no rows, variable values will be undefined. when the statement completes. The static RETURNING INTO clause belongs to a

DELETE, INSERT, or UPDATE statement and the dynamic to the EXECUTE IMMEDIATE statement.

The example below gives a pay decrease to all of the employees with the job ID of PU_CLERK. The affected rows are passed into variables using the RETURNING clause and then displayed with DBMS_OUTPUT.

```
DECLARE
  TYPE t_firstTyp IS TABLE OF hr.employees.first_name%TYPE;
  TYPE t_lastTyp IS TABLE OF hr.employees.last_name%TYPE;
  TYPE t_salTyp IS TABLE OF hr.employees.salary%TYPE;

  t_first      t_firstTyp;
  t_last       t_lastTyp;
  t_sal        t_salTyp;
BEGIN

  UPDATE hr.employees
  SET    salary = salary * .95
  WHERE  job_id = 'PU_CLERK'
  RETURNING first_name, last_name, salary
  BULK COLLECT INTO t_first, t_last, t_sal;

  DBMS_OUTPUT.PUT_LINE ('Updated ' || SQL%ROWCOUNT || '
rows:');

  FOR v_Lp IN t_first.FIRST .. t_first.LAST LOOP
    DBMS_OUTPUT.PUT_LINE (t_first(v_Lp) || ' ' ||
                          t_last(v_Lp) || ' salary ' ||
                          t_sal(v_Lp));
  END LOOP;
END;

Updated 5 rows:
Alexander Khoo salary 2945
Shelli Baida salary 2755
Sigal Tobias salary 2660
Guy Himuro salary 2470
Karen Colmenares salary 2375
```

Creating Triggers

Describe different types of triggers and their uses

Triggers, like stored procedures, are a named PL/SQL unit stored in the database. However, the two are invoked in a very different fashion. Triggers can enabled and disabled, but not explicitly invoked. Triggers are defined with 'triggering events' and will fire whenever that event occurs and the trigger is enabled. If disabled, it does not fire whether or not the event occurs. Triggers are defined on the items. The item may be a table, a view, a schema, or the database. The timing of when the trigger fires is also defined, and may be before or after the triggering event. There are two broad classes of database triggers:

- **DML** -- DML triggers are created on a table or view. They will have a triggering event that is composed of the DML statements DELETE, INSERT, and UPDATE. It is possible to create a MERGE trigger by creating INSERT and UPDATE triggers for statements equivalent to the MERGE operation. DML triggers are further subdivided into Simple (with a single timing point) and compound triggers (that can have multiple timing points).
- **System** -- System triggers are created either on a schema or the database. They will have a triggering event composed of either DDL or database operation statements. DDL triggering events include CREATE, ALTER, and DROP, among others, while system events include options such as STARTUP, SHUTDOWN, AND SERVERERROR.

System triggers can be defined either on the schema or the database:

- **DATABASE** -- The trigger fires whenever any database user initiates the triggering event.
- **SCHEMA** -- The trigger is created on a schema and fires whenever the user who owns it is the current user and initiates the triggering event.

In addition to database triggers, there are application triggers. Instead of being stored in the data dictionary, these are stored (and executed) at the application level. Oracle Forms makes considerable use of application triggers for its functionality. Application triggers will not be covered on the test.

Triggers can perform a broad range of functions in a database. The ability to create code that executes automatically based on certain events allows developers to make a database more responsive. Some of the common uses for database triggers are:

- Populate Primary key values automatically.
- Generate virtual column values.
- Generate log entries for events.
- Generate table access statistics.
- Modify table data when DML statements are issued against views
- Replicate data changes in local tables to tables in a remote database
- Enforce referential integrity when related tables are on different nodes of a distributed database
- Publish information about database events, user events, and SQL statements to subscribing applications
- Restrict DML operations on tables to regular business hours
- Prevent invalid transactions
- Enforce complex business or referential integrity rules that aren't possible with constraints

Create database triggers

The CREATE TRIGGER statement creates or replaces a database trigger, which can be either of these:

- A stored PL/SQL block associated with a table, a schema, or the database

- An anonymous PL/SQL block or an invocation of a procedure implemented in PL/SQL or Java

When the conditions specified in the trigger occur, the trigger is fired automatically. The CREATE TRIGGER statement has a large number of optional components to it. These are necessary to provide the ability to define the specific conditions required for the trigger to be fired. The body of a trigger can contain DML SQL statements. Triggers may contain SELECT statements, but they must be SELECT... INTO... statements or the SELECT statement in the definition of a cursor. DDL and transaction control statements are not allowed in the body of a trigger. System triggers can issue {CREATE/ALTER/DROP} TABLE statements and ALTER...COMPILE operations. The basic syntax to create a trigger is:

```
CREATE TRIGGER trigger_name
BEFORE | AFTER | INSTEAD OF
trigger_event1 [OR trigger_event2 OR trigger_event3]
ON object_name
[REFERENCING OLD AS old / NEW as new]
[FOR EACH ROW]
[WHEN (condition)]
BEGIN
  trigger_body
[EXCEPTION]
END [trigger_name];

trigger_event = INSERT | UPDATE [OF column_list] | DELETE
```

- **Statement-level triggers** -- Fire one time when the triggering statement is executed. They are the default option when creating a trigger.
- **Row-level triggers** -- Fire one time for each row affected by a statement (if no rows are affected, they will not fire). They are created using the FOR EACH ROW clause in the CREATE TRIGGER statement.

A DML trigger is either simple or compound. A simple DML trigger fires at only one of four timing points:

- Before the triggering statement runs
- After the triggering statement runs
- Before each row that the triggering statement affects
- After each row that the triggering statement affects

A compound DML trigger created on a table or editioning view can fire at one or more of the timing points available to simple triggers. When simple or compound DML triggers fire at the row level, they can access the data in the row being processed. With the exception of INSTEAD OF triggers, triggers fired on an UPDATE can include a column list. When a column list is provided, the trigger fires only when one or more of the specified columns are updated. When no column list is provided, the trigger fires when any column in the table is updated.

The triggering event of DML triggers can be composed of more than one triggering statements. Conditional predicates allow the trigger to determine which statement was the source of the current execution. The predicates are referenced as a BOOLEAN expression. The conditional predicates are:

- **INSERTING** -- An INSERT statement fired the trigger.
- **UPDATING** -- An UPDATE statement fired the trigger.
- **UPDATING ('column')** -- An UPDATE statement that affected the specified column fired the trigger.
- **DELETING** -- A DELETE statement fired the trigger.

The below example creates a BEFORE statement trigger named TR_EMPLOYEE_TEST with multiple triggering events for the table HR.EMPLOYEES. It fires whenever there is an INSERT, an UPDATE of the JOB_ID field, or on a DELETE. After creating the trigger, an UPDATE and DELETE operation against the table demonstrate that the trigger fired as expected.

```
CREATE OR REPLACE TRIGGER hr.tr_employee_test
  BEFORE
    INSERT OR
    UPDATE OF job_id OR
    DELETE
  ON hr.employees
  FOR EACH ROW
BEGIN
  CASE
    WHEN INSERTING THEN
      DBMS_OUTPUT.PUT_LINE('Row inserted into employees');
    WHEN UPDATING('JOB_ID') THEN
      DBMS_OUTPUT.PUT_LINE('Updating ' || :OLD.job_id || ' to
' ||
         :NEW.job_id || ' for employee #: ' ||
:OLD.employee_id);
    WHEN DELETING THEN
      DBMS_OUTPUT.PUT_LINE('Deleting employee #: ' ||
:OLD.employee_id);
  END CASE;
END tr_employee_test;


UPDATE hr.employees
SET    job_id = 'IT_PROG'
WHERE employee_id = 102;

Updating AD_VP to IT_PROG for employee #: 102

DELETE FROM hr.employees
WHERE  email = 'KCOLMENA';

Deleting employee #: 119
```

INSTEAD OF triggers are a type of DML trigger created against a view that cannot be updated normally (a noneditioning view), or on a nested table column of a noneditioning view. When a DML statement is issued against the view, the database fires the INSTEAD OF trigger "instead of" running the DML. It is not possible for INSTEAD OF triggers to be conditional. These trigger provide the only means of updating views that cannot be updated directly via DML. The trigger must be designed to determine the intended operation and to perform the equivalent operations on the underlying table(s). INSTEAD OF triggers are always row-level rather than statement-level. They can read the OLD and NEW values, but cannot alter them.

This example creates a BEFORE row trigger with a condition. It will only fire when the JOB_ID field is being updated to AD_VP.

```
CREATE OR REPLACE TRIGGER hr.tr_employee_test
  BEFORE
    UPDATE OF job_id
  ON hr.employees
  FOR EACH ROW
    WHEN (NEW.job_id = 'AD_VP')
BEGIN
  DBMS_OUTPUT.PUT_LINE('Too many chiefs.  Not enough
indians.');
END tr_employee_test;

UPDATE hr.employees
SET    job_id = 'AD_VP'
WHERE employee_id = 120;

Too many chiefs.  Not enough indians.
```

It's also possible to have a trigger invoke a subprogram using the CALL clause. Subprograms invoked using CALL can be implemented in PL/SQL, C, or Java. The CALL functionality is useful if two or more different database triggers perform the exact same code. You can create a procedure with the required code (parameterized if necessary) and have each database trigger execute the new procedure. This reduces redundant code and means any future modifications to the code only occur in one location. The below example creates a procedure called JOB_CHANGE that accepts the old and new JOB_ID values. The previous trigger is then re-engineered to call the new function:

```
CREATE PROCEDURE hr.job_change(p_old_job     VARCHAR2,
                               p_new_job     VARCHAR2)
AS
BEGIN
  IF p_old_job = 'IT_PROG' AND
     p_new_job = 'AD_VP' THEN
    DBMS_OUTPUT.PUT_LINE('What kind of programmer becomes a
VP voluntarily?');
  ELSE
    DBMS_OUTPUT.PUT_LINE('Too many chiefs.  Not enough
indians.');
  END IF;
END job_change;


CREATE OR REPLACE TRIGGER hr.tr_employee_test
  BEFORE
    UPDATE OF job_id
  ON hr.employees
  FOR EACH ROW
    WHEN (NEW.job_id = 'AD_VP')
CALL job_change(:OLD.job_id, :NEW.job_id)

UPDATE hr.employees
SET    job_id='AD_VP'
WHERE  employee_id = 103;

What kind of programmer becomes a VP voluntarily?
```

Manage triggers

The CREATE TRIGGER statement will create a trigger as enabled by default. It is possible to create a trigger in the disabled state by using the DISABLE keyword. Triggers that are created in the disabled state can be tested for compile-time errors before they are enabled. In addition, you might want to temporarily disable triggers for several reasons:

- The object the trigger refers to is temporarily unavailable.
- There is going to be a large data load against the table that you would like to have run without firing triggers.

- The existing data in the table is being reloaded and the trigger would make unwanted changes (i.e. a trigger that generates a primary key using a sequence).

A single trigger can be enabled or disabled using the ALTER TRIGGER statement:

```
ALTER TRIGGER [schema.]trigger_name { ENABLE | DISABLE };
```

All of the triggers on a single table can be enabled or disabled using the ALTER TABLE statement:

```
ALTER TABLE [schema].table_name { ENABLE | DISABLE } ALL
TRIGGERS;
```

The schema in both statements must be the name of the schema containing the trigger. If not supplied, it will default to the current schema.

An invalid trigger can be recompiled using the ALTER TRIGGER statement:

```
ALTER TRIGGER trigger_name COMPILE;
```

To remove unwanted triggers, you use the DROP TRIGGER statement:

```
DROP TRIGGER trigger_name;
```

It is not possible to change the code of a trigger using the ALTER TRIGGER statement. ALTER TRIGGER only allows you to enable, disable, compile, or rename a trigger. You can replace a trigger using the CREATE TRIGGER statement with the OR REPLACE clause. Alternately, you can re-create a trigger by dropping it with the DROP TRIGGER statement and then creating it with the CREATE TRIGGER statement.

You can view information about triggers using the USER_TRIGGERS view (or the ALL_TRIGGERS or DBA_TRIGGERS views):

```
SELECT trigger_body
FROM   all_triggers
WHERE  trigger_name = 'TR_EMPLOYEE_TEST';

TRIGGER_BODY
------------------------------------------------------------
BEGIN
  CASE
    WHEN INSERTING THEN
      DBMS_OUTPUT.PUT_LINE('Row inserted into employees');
    WHEN UPDATING('JOB_ID') THEN
      DBMS_OUTPUT.PUT_LINE('Updating ' || :OLD.job_id ||
         ' to ' || :NEW.job_id || ' for employee #: ' ||
         :OLD.employee_id);
    WHEN DELETING THEN
      DBMS_OUTPUT.PUT_LINE('Deleting employee #: ' ||
                           :OLD.employee_id);
  END CASE;
END tr_employee_test;
```

Creating Compound, DDL, and Event Database Triggers

Compound Triggers

Whereas a simple trigger fires at a single timing point, a compound DML trigger can fire at multiple timing points. Each timing point will have a section with an executable part and optionally an exception-handler. All parts of the trigger have access to a common PL/SQL state. This state is established at the start of the triggering statement and expires when the triggering statement completes (either successfully or with an exception). Any variables and subprograms in the optional declaration part of a compound trigger are accessible to all timing-point sections. When fired, the declarative part of the trigger runs before any of the timing-point sections. Compound triggers can fire up to four times for a single statement:

- **BEFORE STATEMENT** -- Before the triggering statement runs
- **AFTER STATEMENT** -- After the triggering statement runs
- **BEFORE EACH ROW** -- Before each row that the triggering statement affects
- **AFTER EACH ROW** --After each row that the triggering statement affects

Compound triggers for views can only have an INSTEAD OF EACH row section, so they are not truly compound. A compound DML trigger must have at least one timing-point section. If it has multiple timing-point sections, they can be in any order, but no timing-point section can be repeated. Nothing will happen for any timing-point sections that are absent. If a compound DML trigger has no BEFORE or AFTER STATEMENT sections and the triggering statement affects no rows, then the trigger will not fire.

Compound triggers have the following restrictions:

- OLD, NEW, and PARENT cannot appear in the declarative part, the BEFORE STATEMENT section, or the AFTER STATEMENT section.
- The value of NEW can be changed only in the BEFORE EACH ROW section.
- Exceptions can be handled only in the timing-point sections where they occurred.
- GOTO statement targets must be in the same timing-point section.

The example below is a compound trigger that fires at all four execution points. When an UPDATE statement changes the salary for the three employees with the AD_VP job ID, you can see that the BEFORE and AFTER STATEMENT sections each fire once while the row-level sections each fire three times:

```
CREATE OR REPLACE TRIGGER hr.tr_compound_example
  FOR UPDATE OF salary ON hr.employees
    COMPOUND TRIGGER

    v_oldsal     NUMBER;
    v_newsal     NUMBER;
    v_emp        VARCHAR2(40);

BEFORE STATEMENT
IS
BEGIN
  DBMS_OUTPUT.PUT_LINE('Beginning statement');
END BEFORE STATEMENT;

BEFORE EACH ROW
IS
BEGIN
  DBMS_OUTPUT.PUT_LINE('Before updating row');
END BEFORE EACH ROW;

AFTER EACH ROW
IS
BEGIN
```

```
  v_oldsal := :OLD.salary;
  v_newsal := :NEW.salary;
  v_emp    := :OLD.first_name || ' ' || :OLD.last_name;
  DBMS_OUTPUT.PUT_LINE('UPDATING salary for ' || v_emp || '
from ' ||
                       v_oldsal || ' to ' || v_newsal);
  DBMS_OUTPUT.PUT_LINE('Finished updating row');
  DBMS_OUTPUT.PUT_LINE('---------------------');
END AFTER EACH ROW;

AFTER STATEMENT
IS
BEGIN
  DBMS_OUTPUT.PUT_LINE('Ending statement');
END AFTER STATEMENT;

END tr_compound_example;


UPDATE hr.employees
SET    salary = salary * 1.05
WHERE  job_id = 'AD_VP';

Beginning statement
Before updating row
UPDATING salary for Neena Kochhar from 17000 to 17850
Finished updating row
---------------------
Before updating row
UPDATING salary for Lex De Haan from 17000 to 17850
Finished updating row
---------------------
Before updating row
UPDATING salary for Alexander Hunold from 9000 to 9450
Finished updating row
---------------------
Ending statement
```

Create triggers on DDL statements

DDL triggers are created as system triggers and therefore must be created either at the schema or database level. When created at the schema level, the trigger will fire whenever the user that owns the trigger initiates the triggering event. If any other user performs that event, the trigger will not fire. By contrast, a database-level trigger will fire whenever any user initiates the event. The example below creates a trigger against the PLEASE_CHANGEME table in the HR schema. The user OCPGURU then issues an ALTER TABLE statement against the table and the trigger does not fire.

```
CREATE TABLE please_changeme (
col1      NUMBER);

CREATE OR REPLACE TRIGGER tr_hr_noalter
BEFORE ALTER ON hr.SCHEMA
BEGIN
  RAISE_APPLICATION_ERROR (
    num => -20001,
    msg => 'HR Cannot alter objects');
END;

ALTER TABLE please_changeme ADD (col2 NUMBER);
table PLEASE_CHANGEME altered.
```

In the below example, the previous schema-level trigger is dropped and a new one created on the OCPGURU schema. The alter table statement is attempted again and this time fails with the supplied error.

```
DROP TRIGGER tr_hr_noalter;
CREATE OR REPLACE TRIGGER tr_ocpguru_noalter
BEFORE ALTER ON ocpguru.SCHEMA
BEGIN
  RAISE_APPLICATION_ERROR (
    num => -20001,
    msg => 'OCPGuru Cannot alter objects');
END;

ALTER TABLE please_changeme ADD (col3 NUMBER);
ORA-20001: OCPGuru Cannot alter objects
```

Create triggers on system events

System events are particular database states that can be used to fire a system trigger. Unless otherwise noted, it is possible to create triggers for these events at either the DATABASE or SCHEMA level. When a triggering event occurs, the database will open an autonomous transaction scope, fire the trigger, and commit any transaction imbedded in the trigger (without affecting any existing user transaction in the triggering session).

The available system events are:

- **AFTER STARTUP** -- Causes the database to fire the trigger whenever the database is opened. This event is valid only with DATABASE, not with SCHEMA.
- **BEFORE SHUTDOWN** -- Causes the database to fire the trigger whenever an instance of the database is shut down. This event is valid only with DATABASE, not with SCHEMA.
- **AFTER DB_ROLE_CHANGE** -- In a Data Guard configuration, causes the database to fire the trigger whenever a role change occurs from standby to primary or from primary to standby. This event is valid only with DATABASE, not with SCHEMA.
- **AFTER SERVERERROR** -- Causes the database to fire the trigger whenever a server error message is logged. There are a handful of database errors that will not raise this event. See the PL/SQL Language Reference for details.
- **AFTER LOGON** -- Causes the database to fire the trigger whenever a client application logs onto the database.
- **BEFORE LOGOFF** -- Causes the database to fire the trigger whenever a client application logs off the database.
- **AFTER SUSPEND** -- Causes the database to fire the trigger whenever a server error causes a transaction to be suspended.

The example below makes use of the AFTER SERVERERROR to fire a trigger when an ORA-1722 error is raised:

```
CREATE OR REPLACE TRIGGER tr_nota_number
AFTER SERVERERROR ON DATABASE
BEGIN
  IF (IS_SERVERERROR (1722)) THEN
    DBMS_OUTPUT.PUT_LINE('Someone doesn''t know what a number
is again');
  END IF;
END;

INSERT INTO hr.departments
VALUES (400, 'New Department', 'A14', '5345');

Error report:
SQL Error: ORA-01722: invalid number

Someone doesn't know what a number is again
```

The example below makes use of the AFTER LOGON to fire a trigger that adds a record to a table to audit user logins after a database logon occurs:

```
CREATE OR REPLACE TRIGGER tr_logon
AFTER LOGON ON DATABASE
BEGIN
  INSERT INTO audit_users
  VALUES (USER, SYSDATE);
END;

CONNECT ocpguru/[password]

SELECT * FROM audit_users;

USERNAME                       LOGON_TIME
------------------------------ ----------
OCPGURU                        01-JUL-12
```

Using the PL/SQL Compiler

Describe the new PL/SQL compiler and features

There have been several enhancements made to the PL/SQL compiler in versions 10G and 11G. Some of the compiler enhancements include:

Automatic Subprogram Inlining

Subprogram inlining replaces the invocation of a subprogram in the same PL/SQL unit with a copy of the invoked subprogram. Doing so almost always improves program performance. The PRAGMA INLINE clause specifies whether individual subprogram invocations should be inlined or not. It is also possible to turn on automatic inlining by setting the compilation parameter PLSQL_OPTIMIZE_LEVEL to 3 (the default is 2). Setting the level to 3 tells the compiler to search for inlining opportunities automatically. In cases where automatic inlining does not improve program performance, the PL/SQL hierarchical profiler can be used to identify subprograms for which to turn off inlining.

PL/Scope

PL/Scope uses the PL/SQL source text to collect and organize data about user-defined identifiers. It is a compiler-driven tool that is used through IDEs such as SQL Developer or JDeveloper. PL/Scope can increase PL/SQL developer productivity by reducing the time spent browsing through source text.

PL/SQL Hierarchical Profiler

The hierarchical profiler reports the dynamic execution profile of your PL/SQL program by subprogram invocations. SQL and PL/SQL execution times are reported separately. It provides information such as number of subprogram invocations, time spent in the subprogram, time spent in the subprogram's descendents, and parent-children information.

PL/SQL Native Compiler

With Oracle 11G, the PL/SQL native compiler now generates native code directly. In previous releases, native compilation translated PL/SQL code to C code and required a C compiler to generate the native code. The execution speed of natively compiled PL/SQL programs can be improved in some cases by an order of magnitude. PL/SQL units can be compiled into native code, which is then stored in the SYSTEM tablespace. Any PL/SQL unit of any type can be compiled into native code. Without native compilation, the statements in a PL/SQL unit are compiled into system code which is stored in the catalog and interpreted at run time.

Use the new PL/SQL compiler initialization parameters

PLSCOPE_SETTINGS

Controls the compile time collection, cross reference, and storage of PL/SQL source code identifier data. PLSCOPE_SETTINGS can be set on a session, system, or per-library unit (ALTER COMPILE) basis. The current setting of PLSCOPE_SETTINGS for any library unit can be attained by querying the *_PLSQL_OBJECT_SETTINGS views. Any identifier data collected by setting this parameter can be accessed using the *_IDENTIFIERS views. Allowable values are:

- **IDENTIFIERS:NONE** -- Disables collection of identifier data. This is the default.
- **IDENTIFIERS:ALL** -- Enables the collection of all source code identifier data.

PLSQL_CODE_TYPE

Specifies the compilation mode for PL/SQL library units. When the value of this parameter is changed, it has no effect on PL/SQL library units that have already been compiled. The value of this parameter is stored persistently with each library unit. If a PL/SQL library unit is compiled native, all subsequent automatic recompilations of that library unit will use native compilation. Allowable values are:

- **INTERPRETED** -- PL/SQL library units will be compiled to PL/SQL bytecode format. Such modules are executed by the PL/SQL interpreter engine. This is the default.
- **NATIVE** -- PL/SQL library units (with the possible exception of top-level anonymous PL/SQL blocks) will be compiled to native (machine) code. Such modules will be executed natively without incurring any interpreter overhead.

PLSQL_OPTIMIZE_LEVEL

Specifies the optimization level that will be used to compile PL/SQL library units. The higher the setting of this parameter, the more effort the compiler will make to optimize the units. As a general rule, setting this parameter to 2 will pay off in better execution performance. Setting this parameter to 1 will result in almost as good a compilation with less use of compile-time resources. Allowable values are:

- **0** -- Maintains the evaluation order of Oracle9i and earlier releases. Also removes the new semantic identity of BINARY_INTEGER and PLS_INTEGER and restores the earlier rules for the evaluation of integer expressions. Use of level 0 will forfeit most of the performance gains of PL/SQL in Oracle Database 10g.
- **1** -- Applies a wide range of optimizations to PL/SQL programs including the elimination of unnecessary computations and exceptions, but generally does not move source code out of its original source order.
- **2** -- Applies a wide range of modern optimization techniques beyond those of level 1 including changes which may move source code relatively far from its original location. This is the default.

- **3** -- Applies a wide range of optimization techniques beyond those of level 2, automatically including techniques not specifically requested.

PLSQL_WARNINGS

Enables or disables the reporting of warning messages by the PL/SQL compiler, and specifies which warning messages to show as errors. Multiple value clauses may be specified, enclosed in quotes and separated by commas. Each value clause is composed of a qualifier, a colon (:), and a modifier. Allowable qualifier values are:

- **ENABLE** -- Enable a specific warning or a set of warnings
- **DISABLE** -- Disable a specific warning or a set of warnings
- **ERROR** -- Treat a specific warning or a set of warnings as errors

Allowable modifier values are:

- **ALL** -- Apply the qualifier to all warning messages
- **SEVERE** -- Apply the qualifier to only those warning messages in the SEVERE category
- **INFORMATIONAL** -- Apply the qualifier to only those warning messages in the INFORMATIONAL category
- **PERFORMANCE** -- Apply the qualifier to only those warning messages in the PERFORMANCE category

An example use of the parameter would be:

```
PLSQL_WARNINGS = 'ENABLE:SEVERE', 'DISABLE:INFORMATIONAL';
```

You can query the view *_PLSQL_OBJECT_SETTINGS to determine the values used when compiling existing PL/SQL objects.

```
DESCRIBE  dba_plsql_object_settings
Name                     Null      Type
-------------------- -------- --------------
OWNER                    NOT NULL VARCHAR2(30)
NAME                     NOT NULL VARCHAR2(30)
TYPE                              VARCHAR2(12)
PLSQL_OPTIMIZE_LEVEL              NUMBER
PLSQL_CODE_TYPE                   VARCHAR2(4000)
PLSQL_DEBUG                       VARCHAR2(4000)
PLSQL_WARNINGS                    VARCHAR2(4000)
NLS_LENGTH_SEMANTICS              VARCHAR2(4000)
PLSQL_CCFLAGS                     VARCHAR2(4000)
PLSCOPE_SETTINGS                  VARCHAR2(4000)
```

Use the new PL/SQL compile time warnings

By default, when compiling PL/SQL, the compiler only reports errors that prevent the code from being compiled successfully. However, the PL/SQL compiler generates (but does not display) warnings for conditions that are not serious enough to prevent compilation. This might be something like code that can never be reached or the use of a PL/SQL feature that has been deprecated. In order to see warnings as well as errors generated during compilation, you can query the static data dictionary view *_ERRORS. Alternately, in SQL*Plus you can use the command SHOW ERRORS. There are three categories of PL/SQL warnings:

- **SEVERE** -- Condition might cause unexpected action or wrong results.
- **PERFORMANCE** -- Condition might cause performance problems.
- **INFORMATIONAL** -- Condition does not affect performance or correctness, but you might want to change it to make the code more maintainable.

If you want to see warnings displayed along with errors by default, you can set the compilation parameter PLSQL_WARNINGS. This parameter allows you to:

- Enable and disable all warnings, one or more categories of warnings, or specific warnings.
- Treat specific warnings as errors that must be corrected before compilation will succeed.

The value of PLSQL_WARNINGS can be set at the following levels:

- **Database** -- When set with the ALTER SYSTEM statement, the parameter is used for the entire database.
- **Session** -- When set with the ALTER SESSION statement, the parameter is used for a given session.
- **PL/SQL unit** -- The ALTER statement can be used with the compiler_parameters clause to set the parameter for a single stored PL/SQL unit.

In any of the preceding ALTER statements, the value of PLSQL_WARNINGS is set with the syntax:

```
PLSQL_WARNINGS = 'value_clause' [, 'value_clause' ] ...
```

Some examples are:

Enable PERFORMANCE warnings for the entire database:

```
ALTER SYSTEM SET PLSQL_WARNINGS='ENABLE:PERFORMANCE';
```

Enable all warnings for the current session:

```
ALTER SESSION SET PLSQL_WARNINGS='ENABLE:ALL';
```

Enable SEVERE warnings and disable INFORMATIONAL warning for the procedure ocp_test:

```
ALTER PROCEDURE ocp_test
COMPILE PLSQL_WARNINGS='ENABLE:SEVERE',
'DISABLE:INFORMATIONAL';
```

Disable all warnings for the current session:

```
ALTER SESSION SET PLSQL_WARNINGS='DISABLE:ALL';
```

DBMS_WARNING

The DBMS_WARNING package allows you to display, set, or alter the value of PLSQL_WARNINGS from a development environment such as SQL*Plus. It can set the parameter at either the database or session level.

- **ADD_WARNING_SETTING_CAT** -- This procedure allows you to modify the current session or system warning category settings with the value supplied. The value will be added to the existing parameter setting if the value for the warning_category or warning_value has not been set, or override the existing value
- **ADD_WARNING_SETTING_NUM** -- This procedure allows you to modify the current session or system warning number settings with the value supplied. If the value was already set, you will override the existing value.
- **GET_CATEGORY** -- This function returns the category name, given the message number.
- **GET_WARNING_SETTING_CAT** -- This function returns the specific warning category setting for the current session.
- **GET_WARNING_SETTING_NUM** -- This function returns the specific warning number setting for the current session.
- **GET_WARNING_SETTING_STRING** -- This function returns the entire warning string for the current session.
- **SET_WARNING_SETTING_STRING** -- This procedure replaces previous settings with the new value. The warning string may contain a mix of category and warning numbers using the same syntax as used when issuing an ALTER SESSION or SYSTEM SET PLSQL_WARNINGS command.

Managing PL/SQL Code

Describe and use conditional compilation

Conditional compilation is designed to allow you to create code that will compile under multiple versions of the Oracle database, using only the features appropriate to the release it is being compiled under. When compiled under a release where a particular PL/SQL feature does not exist, the compiler automatically disables it. It is also possible to activate or deactivate debugging statements when code is compiled in a development or production environment respectively. This guide outlines how conditional compilation works. To actually learn to use conditional compilation, you should refer to the Oracle PL/SQL Language Reference. It is not a topic that would translate well in an abbreviated form. The main elements that make up conditional compilation are:

- **Preprocessor control token** -- Identifies code that is processed before the PL/SQL unit is compiled. The syntax is: $plsql_identifier. There cannot be space between $ and plsql_identifier.
- **Selection Directive** -- Similar to an IF statement, a selection directive selects source text to compile.
- **Inquiry Directive** -- Provides information about the compilation environment. The syntax is: $$name.
- **Error Directive** -- Produces a user-defined error message during compilation. The syntax is: $ERROR varchar2_static_expression $END.

Source PL/SQL text is identified for compilation using selection directives. A selection directive condition will usually include an inquiry directive. All conditional compilation directives are built from preprocessor control tokens and PL/SQL text. The syntax for selection directives is:

```
$IF boolean_static_expression $THEN
  text
[ $ELSIF boolean_static_expression $THEN
  text
]...
[ $ELSE
  text
$END
]
```

The text can be anything, but typically, it is either a statement or an error directive. The selection directive evaluates the BOOLEAN static expressions in the order that they appear until either one expression has the value TRUE or the list of expressions is exhausted. An inquiry directive is normally part of the BOOLEAN expression. If one expression has the value TRUE, its text is compiled, the remaining expressions are not evaluated, and their text is not analyzed. If no expression has the value TRUE, then if $ELSE is present, its text is compiled; otherwise, no text is compiled.

The DBMS_DB_VERSION package can be used to provide the information required for conditional compilation to make version-specific decisions. It provides these static constants:

- The PLS_INTEGER constant VERSION identifies the current Oracle Database version.
- The PLS_INTEGER constant RELEASE identifies the current Oracle Database release number.
- Each BOOLEAN constant of the form VER_LE_v has the value TRUE if the database version is less than or equal to v; otherwise, it has the value FALSE.
- Each BOOLEAN constant of the form VER_LE_v_r has the value TRUE if the database version is less than or equal to v and release is less than or equal to r; otherwise, it has the value FALSE.
- All constants representing Oracle Database 10g or earlier have the value FALSE.

Hide PL/SQL source code using dynamic obfuscation and the Wrap utility

Wrapping stored PL/SQL objects prevents the source text from being displayed with the static data dictionary views *_SOURCE. This provides some level of protection for your code from being read. However, there are utilities available that can access wrapped PL/SQL, so it should not be considered a high-security protection method. You can wrap the source text for any of the following object types:

- Package specification
- Package body
- Type specification
- Type body
- Function
- Procedure

It is possible to create a wrapped file with either the PL/SQL Wrapper utility or a DBMS_DDL subprogram. The PL/SQL Wrapper utility uses a SQL file as input. The DBMS_DDL subprograms will wrap the source text of single dynamically generated wrappable PL/SQL unit. Wrapped files are always upward-compatible between Oracle releases.

Limitations

- Wrapped files are not downward-compatible between releases.
- Wrapping PL/SQL source text is not a secure way to hide passwords or table names.
- You cannot wrap the PL/SQL source text of triggers.

Guidelines

- Wrap only the body of a package or type, not the specification.

- Wrap files only after you have finished editing them. You cannot edit wrapped files.
- Before distributing a wrapped file, view it in a text editor and ensure that all important parts are wrapped.

The PL/SQL wrapper utility takes a single SQL file and produces an equivalent text file in which the PL/SQL source text of each wrappable PL/SQL unit is wrapped. The wrapper utility does not connect to the database. The utility is an executable file run from the OS command line. The syntax to wrap a file from the OS command line is (with no spaces around the equal signs):

```
wrap iname=input_file [ oname=output_file ]
```

- **input_file** -- The name of the file that contains any combination of SQL statements.
- **output_file** -- The name of the wrapped file that the utility will create.

The default file extension for input_file is sql. The default name of output_file is input_file.plb. The output file can be run as a script in SQL*Plus.

DBMS_DDL

The DBMS_DDL package has two subprograms that will produce wrapped output:

DBMS_DDL.WRAP -- This function takes as input a single CREATE OR REPLACE statement that specifies creation of a PL/SQL package specification, package body, function, procedure, type specification or type body and returns a CREATE OR REPLACE statement where the text of the PL/SQL unit has been obfuscated.

DBMS_DDL.CREATE_WRAPPED -- The procedure takes as input a single CREATE OR REPLACE statement that specifies creation of a PL/SQL package specification, package body, function, procedure, type specification or type body. It then generates a CREATE OR REPLACE statement with the PL/SQL source text obfuscated and executes the generated statement. In effect, this procedure bundles together the operations of wrapping the text and creating the PL/SQL unit.

Managing Dependencies

Track and manage procedural dependencies

Some database objects reference other objects as part of their definition. A view is the classic example, as it is defined by a query that references tables or other views. Likewise stored subprograms can include SQL statements that reference tables or call other stored subprograms. If the definition of object A includes a reference to object B, then A is a dependent object (of B) and B is a referenced object (of A).

The *_DEPENDENCIES views can be used to find the object dependencies that exist in the database. The following two queries display information about the dependencies that the OCPGURU schema has on the HR schema:

```
SELECT name, referenced_name, referenced_type
FROM   user_dependencies
WHERE  type = 'PROCEDURE'
AND    referenced_owner = 'HR'

NAME            REFERENCED_NAME REFERENCED_TYPE
--------------- --------------- ---------------
GET_EMPLOYEE    EMPLOYEES        TABLE
EMP_YEARS       EMPLOYEES        TABLE
EMPS_DS         EMPLOYEES        TABLE


SELECT DISTINCT type, referenced_name, referenced_type
FROM   user_dependencies
WHERE  referenced_owner = 'HR'

TYPE           REFERENCED_NAME    REFERENCED_TYPE
-------------- ------------------ ----------------
SYNONYM        DEPARTMENTS         TABLE
PACKAGE BODY   EMPLOYEES           TABLE
PROCEDURE      EMPLOYEES           TABLE
```

When the definition of a referenced object is changed, this may prevent dependent objects from functioning. For example, if a table is dropped, then any view that queries that table can no longer function. Dependencies can be either direct or indirect. If object A depends on object B, which depends on object C, then A is a direct dependent of B, B is a direct dependent of C, and A is an indirect dependent of C. The type of dependency is important because direct dependents are invalidated only when changes to the referenced object affect them. By contrast, indirect dependents can be invalidated by changes to the reference object that do not affect them. If a change to C invalidates B, it also invalidates A. This is cascading invalidation.

Invalidation of objects can be either coarse or fine-grained:

- **Coarse-grained invalidation** -- Any DDL statement that changes a referenced object invalidates all of its dependents.
- **Fine-grained invalidation** -- A DDL statement that changes a referenced object invalidates only dependents for which the dependent relies on the attribute that the DDL changed or the compiled metadata of the dependent is no longer correct for the changed referenced object.

If an object is not valid when it is referenced, it must be validated before being used. Validation occurs automatically when an object is referenced. When an object is invalidated, on the next access, the compiler will attempt to recompile. If it recompiles without errors, it is revalidated; otherwise, it will remain invalid.

When a local subprogram is compiled with a dependency on a remote subprogram, the compilation timestamp of the remote subprogram is stored in the object code of the local subprogram. Any time that the local subprogram is executed, the recorded compilation timestamp of the remote subprogram will be compared to the current timestamp. If the current timestamp is later than the date stored in the local subprogram's object code, an error will result. The local subprogram will be marked invalid. If it is executed a second time, the subprogram will successfully recompile and the new timestamp of the remote subprogram will be stored in the local subprogram's object code. To avoid errors of this nature, you should always manually recompile any local subprograms with remote dependencies after the remote subprogram has recompiled.

To reduce invalidation of dependent objects, you should follow these guidelines:

- Add new items to the end of the package. This preserves the entry point numbers of existing top-level package items, preventing their invalidation.
- Reference tables indirectly, using views. This enables you to add columns to the table without invalidating dependent views or dependent PL/SQL objects. You can also modify or delete columns not referenced by the view without invalidating dependent objects. Issuing a CREATE OR REPLACE VIEW does not invalidate an existing view or its dependents if the new ROWTYPE matches the old ROWTYPE.

ABOUT THE AUTHOR

Matthew Morris is an Oracle Database Administrator and Developer currently employed as a Database Engineer with Computer Sciences Corporation. Matthew has worked with the Oracle database since 1996 when he worked in the RDBMS support team for Oracle Support Services. Employed with Oracle for over eleven years in support and development positions, Matthew was an early adopter of the Oracle Certified Professional program. He was one of the first one hundred Oracle Certified Database Administrators (version 7.3) and in the first hundred to become an Oracle Certified Forms Developer. In the years since, he has upgraded his Database Administrator certification for releases 8i, 9i, 10G and 11G, added the Application Express and SQL Expert certifications, and the PL/SQL Developer Certified Associate certification. Outside of Oracle, he has CompTIA certifications in Linux+ and Security+.

45113500R10101

Made in the USA
Middletown, DE
24 June 2017